D0915323

Ezra Pound

THE LONDON YEARS:
1908–1920

Ezra Pound

THE LONDON YEARS:
1908—1920

Edited by
PHILIP GROVER

AMS PRESS
NEW YORK

ST. PHILIPS COLLEGE LIBRARY

Library of Congress Cataloging in Publication Data

Ezra Pound Conference, 1st, Sheffield University, 1976.
  Ezra Pound: the London years, 1908–1920.

  Includes bibliographical references and index.
  1. Pound, Ezra Loomis, 1885–1972—Congresses.
I. Grover, Philip.
PS3531.082Z489   1978   811'.5'2   77-78316
ISBN 0-404-16006-9

811·52

E99

COPYRIGHT 1978 BY AMS PRESS, INC.

ALL RIGHTS RESERVED

PRINTED IN THE UNITED STATES OF AMERICA

FIRST AMS PRESS EDITION: 1978

ACKNOWLEDGMENTS:

New Directions Publishing Corp.: Ezra Pound, from *Personae,* Copyright © 1926
by Ezra Pound. From *The Literary Essays of Ezra Pound,* Copyright © 1918, 1920,
1925 by Ezra Pound; all rights reserved. From *The Spirit of Romance,* Copyright ©
1968 by Ezra Pound; all rights reserved. From *Selected Prose 1909–1965,*
Copyright © 1973 by the Estate of Ezra Pound; all rights reserved.

Faber and Faber Limited: Ezra Pound, from *Collected Shorter Poems;* from *The Spirit
of Romance* and postcard sent by Pound to Mrs. Pound 29 May 1919, reprinted by
permission of the Ezra Pound Literary Property Trust and Faber & Faber Ltd.

Previously unpublished material by Ezra Pound, Copyright © 1978 by the Trustees of the Ezra Pound Literary Property Trust.

Cover: Pen and ink drawing of Ezra Pound and signature by Wyndham Lewis,
1914; reproduced by permission of Omar Pound.

ST. PHILIPS COLLEGE LIBRARY

NOTE TO THE READER

Five of the six essays in this book were first read at the Pound Conference held at the University of Sheffield from 23 April to 13 May 1976. (The exception is Pratt's "Ezra Pound and the Image;" see preface, page xii). Following the essays is the Exhibit Catalogue, which has been reproduced from a copy of the original, reduced to fit, with the pages rearranged to provide a more pleasing typographical appearance in this format. The texts of Canto IV, "Near Perigord," and "Provincia Deserta," reprinted in the original catalogue, have been omitted from this edition.

60520

Contents

Illustrations

Contributors

WALTER BAUMANN is a Senior Lecturer in Modern Languages at the New University of Ulster, Coleraine, Northern Ireland. He is the author of *The Rose in the Steel Dust: An Examination of the Cantos of Ezra Pound*, published by Francke Verlag, Berne (1967), and by the University of Miami Press (1970). He contributed an article entitled "Secretary of Nature, J. Heydon" to Eva Hesse's *New Approaches to Ezra Pound* (1969), and has written on Ezra Pound in *Seminar* and the *Journal of English and Germanic Philology*. He has also published articles on Max Frisch and Hermann Broch and is currently studying certain themes in Pound's Cantos and working on Goethe.

IAN BELL was educated at the University of Reading where he did his doctoral dissertation on Pound's literary criticism. He has published articles on nineteenth century American intellectual history and on Ezra Pound, including one on "Hugh Selwyn Mauberley" in a recent issue of *Paideuma*. He is a Lecturer in American Literature at the University of Keele.

ERIC HOMBERGER is a graduate of the University of California at Berkeley, the University of Chicago, and Cambridge University where his doctoral dissertation was on Pound's work up to 1920. He is the co-editor of *The Cambridge Mind* (1970), editor of *Ezra Pound: The Critical Heritage* (1972), and author of *The Art of the Real: Poetry in England and America since 1939* (1977). He is currently at work on a long essay on war memorials. He is Lecturer in American Literature at the University of East Anglia, Norwich, and will be visiting professor at the University of Minnesota in 1977–78.

ix

PETER MAKIN's book, *Provence and Pound,* will be published by
the University of California Press in 1978. He has taught in West
Africa and Japan, and is presently a Lecturer in the Department
of English and Comparative Studies at the University of Warwick.

DONALD MONK is a lecturer in the Department of American
Studies at the University of Manchester, where his doctoral dissertation was on poetic theory in Pound, Eliot, and Yeats. He has
published on Pound's Cantos in the *Journal of American Studies,*
and is completing a book on twentieth-century American poetry
entitled *Declarations of Independence.*

WILLIAM PRATT is a professor of English at Miami (Ohio)
University. He has edited *The Imagist Poem* (1963), *The Fugitive
Poets* (1965), and *The College Writer* (1969), has published poems
and translations and essays on poets and poetry. He was Fulbright
Professor of American Literature at University College, Dublin,
and in the fall of 1976 was Resident Scholar at the Miami University Center in Luxembourg.

Preface

In April 1976 the first Ezra Pound Conference in England took place at Sheffield University. This was, to a large extent, a happy accident. I had decided that to celebrate the American Bicentennial, rather than have yet one more exhibition about the American Revolution, it would be more interesting to focus on some American poets who had had some important literary associations with England. With this in mind I approached Omar Pound whom I had known for some time through having taught with him at the Cambridgeshire College of Arts and Technology before I moved up to Sheffield in 1969. Omar, I knew, had various books that might be of interest and he also was acquainted with a number of contemporary American and British poets. I did not know, however, what treasures were to be revealed. For as we sat talking one evening he produced for me a xerox copy of a manuscript. "Good God! This is part of the Fourth Canto!" Thus the idea to mount an exhibition exclusively devoted to Ezra Pound was born in Omar's house one night in the late summer of 1975. Over the next nine months we worked out in detail what was to go into the exhibition. On the canvas backs of old maps, one of the United States, Omar had drawn out the size of the exhibition cases we were to use. Sitting on the floor with these in front of me we would arrange and rearrange, selecting and rejecting, what was to go into the exhibition. Much that could have been included had to be left out as it was redundant or did not fit into the overall theme of the exhibition. Omar's generosity throughout was truly astonishing—as was the patience of his wife Elizabeth as I came back again and again to commandeer her living-room floor and occupy the guest room.

From the exhibition then came the idea to have a conference that would deal with the same period of time and the same themes. Pound studies in England were then in an unorganised state: who were the other Poundians? Of course there were certain well-known names: Donald Davie, but he was in America; Christine Brooke-Rose, but she was in Paris and replied that she was too engaged with her duties as Chairman of her Department and that she was now working on entirely different subjects; Denis Donoghue, who was to have given us a paper but in the end was unable to do so. But there were others whom I knew or learnt about and gradually the Conference too began to take shape and become a reality. It had a greater success than I could have dreamt for it. Obviously, the chance of getting together and discussing with colleagues—even discovering *who* one's Poundian colleagues were—was something a number of us had been waiting for. Many, if not all, found themselves in departments where they were the only ones interested in Pound. Each was pursuing a lonely path of scholarly and critical interest without comment or communication with others. The conference brought us together. And this Conference begat others. Already there has been a second Pound Conference held at Keele University in September 1976, and by the time this book goes to press a third will have taken place in London in September 1977. So something was started at Sheffield, something that may well turn out to have been of some modest importance in the development of Pound studies in England.

The general theme of the exhibition was the literary activity of Pound in London between 1908 and 1920. This is also the major concern of the first two essays, which I will discuss below; the remaining essays consider in much more detail some of these activities and literary productions and here too complement the physical exhibits that were on view at the conference. There, for example, we showed Pound's copy of the *Poetical Works of Lionel Johnson*—with his preface—and his copy of *The Poems of Ernest Dowson.* On the rear end-paper of this volume Pound had copied out Victor Prarr's "Epitaphium Citharistriae." Although we showed the copy Dorothy had given to her mother, Olivia Shakespear, of Johnson's *Post Liminium,* Pound had his own copy with his Kensington address inscribed within (see catalogue entries 14-17).

Pound found his way into the Edwardian literary scene partly through his future mother-in-law who was a first cousin to Lionel Johnson and a novelist in her own right. She it was who introduced Pound to Yeats. Both she and Dorothy were interested too in Chinese poetry before they met Pound. The circle around Olivia brought Pound into contact with Maurice Hewlett whom Pound visited one Christmas, a visit evoked in Canto LXXX along with much else and many other friends of this time in London.

Another Edwardian figure is Allen Upward (b. 1863) whose *Odes of Confucius* and *The Sayings of Kung the Master* were published in The Wisdon of the East series as was *The Flight of the Dragon* by Laurence Binyon (1911). Upward's sayings of Kung appeared in *The New Freewoman* in November and December 1913; a number of them are markedly similar to those used by Pound, particularly in Canto XIII.

One person who is only briefly mentioned by a number of the contributors is Wyndham Lewis (who needs to be remembered in any account of this period of Pound's life for more than being kicked downstairs by Hulme). Lewis, *Blast,* Gaudier-Brzeska and the Vortex receive only passing reference; their importance is much greater than the space here given to them, particularly in the formation of Pound's concept of the image and its relations to painting and ar-

chitecture as well as poetry. I hope to be able to fill this gap
sometime in the not too distant future.

The essays in this book were all, with one exception,
given at the Sheffield conference. The exception is the
paper by Professor William Pratt. He was at the conference,
but this paper was presented on a lecture tour in Scotland
that same spring and again to the conference at Keele.
However, since it deals with a general theme central to the
1908-1920 period, I asked his permission to include it.

Both the Pratt essay and the one by Dr. Eric Homberger help define more precisely what we ought to understand by Modernism. Homberger is interested in what were
Modernism's relationships to the earlier literary cultures of
England and France; Pratt seeks to define some of the
distinctive features of imagism. Imagism, he argues, is
when literature became distinctly modern. And to a large
extent, Pratt goes on to say, Pound *was* Modernism. Imagism is not just a passing phase, a fashion, it is central to the
whole modernist movement. The imagist poem develops
from the static, spatial, descriptive poem to the dynamic,
satirical and ironic. And it is related to all those attempts of
modernism to find the immanence in the visible world, a
view that has important religious overtones for nearly all
the writers, although the religious implications may be quite
at variance with each other. He concludes his examination
with a list of five attributes that characterize not only the
image as Pound understood it but also the modern style.

Pratt points out, as does Homberger, the important
connections with French poetry and Pound's critical use of
the *Symbolistes*. One might only add that Pound's belief in an
"absolute rhythm" and his linking of this to "a like belief in a
sort of permanent metaphor" is probably part of his heritage derived from Flaubert, for these are ideas one can
easily find in Flaubert's correspondence. Both Pratt and
Homberger show that literary history properly understood
is also criticism, and highly illuminating criticism too.

After these general considerations come some more detailed examinations of particular aspects of Pound's poetic progress from 1908–1920.

Donald Monk takes a somewhat different view of the centrality of the image to that taken by William Pratt. I have not tried to eliminate these differences and make the papers take a consistent "line". These are scholars talking to each other and disagreement is of the essence of scholarly conversation. But above all Monk concentrates on the Provençal tradition and its place in Pound's theories of language and the history of poetry. From history we proceed, as always with Pound, to poetic practice. Monk examines in detail three of Pound's efforts at "translation" or evocation: Bertrans de Born, Rihaku, and Sextus Propertius. It is on the creative use of "mistranslations" that his attention falls. What comes out of this probing is Pound's immense vitality, his creative energy. The past for Pound is being re-created, being made new, available to us through his own immense intelligence, but more, his poetic gift which is intimately—inevitably for Pound—linked to his life-time efforts at technique.

Peter Makin, too, devotes himself to a study of Pound and Provence. In doing so he explores a quite new area: the Latin poetry of medieval Christianity and Pound's uses and refusals to use parts of it. In the course of Makin's argument Remy de Gourmont appears an important intermediary for Pound's ideas and choice of authors to translate even if, as so often in Pound, his use of these is unscholarly, nay reckless and cavalier. Exactly what uses he made and did not make of Gourmont's *Le Latin mystique* is a complex subject that Makin subtly disentangles. The essay is a contribution to our understanding of how Pound made creative use of fragments of the past, creating new patterns, new insights and syntheses. The author rightly, to my mind, emphasizes that when Pound starts from an aesthetic perception and makes historic deductions he is invariably right—or at least convincing. The rot sets in when he tries to be historically more respectable and uses historical evidence to re-create the sense of a period. Makin's effort is to broaden our understanding of the context in which Pound's choice of the troubadours' Paideuma and his religion of light and illumination was made.

A similar contextual study is presented by Ian Bell for "Hugh Selwyn Mauberley." He does this by a close examination of the vocabulary of the poem, particularly the section "Mauberley 1920." Since so much of this is scientific we are led into an examination of a whole complex of scientific ideas that were current and on which Pound could draw for his delineation of Mauberley. This essay too takes us back to Pound's Edwardian London for some of its developments and arguments.

Finally Walter Baumann gives us a very detailed examination of "Canto IV," starting with the metrics of the poem and going on to examine larger and larger structures. In his examination of the vocabulary of the poem he notices something which Hugh Witemeyer has also recently pointed out to me and which deserves a fuller treatment in Pound's whole work: the absence of finite verbs. This does not accord well with Pound's remarks on the centrality of verbs. The action is in the nouns and present participles, but many lines have no verbal formation at all.

The two roofs: "a fish-scale roof" and "the church roof in Poictiers", which Baumann discusses are of course one and the same roof, that of Notre-Dame-la-Grande. (See catalogue entry 5.) For "Canto IV" very firmly returns us to the material of the exhibition, including not only part of the manuscript but also the earliest printed versions of the poem. And although he does not say so, his examination of "Canto IV" provides us with a detailed illustration of a long imagist poem, thus taking us back to the analyses developed in William Pratt's paper. Baumann's essay also carried us forward into *The Cantos* as a whole, to the poetry that Pound was to devote his life to after 1920 and the break with England.

Eric Homberger

Modernists and Edwardians

The Edwardians have been berated for their insularity and smugness, for their narrow chauvinism and philistinism. One might well think that they spent most of their time reading romancers like Maurice Hewlett, W. H. Hudson and Kenneth Grahame, or attending performances of *Peter Pan,* when they were not busy arranging for the prosecution of free spirits like Wells and Lawrence, and writing letters to *The Times* urging stricter censorship. This view, or something like it, has been a source of minor academic amusement. There is nothing quite so flattering as someone else's blindness and failures of taste. So we go back to early notices of Pound and Eliot, dig up obscure attacks on the Imagists, or hostile, uncomprehending reviews of *The Waste Land,* and have not resisted the temptation to accept the literary history of the Edwardian years as seen through the eyes of the persecuted but ultimately victorious party. There is a strikingly close parallel in the way the success of the underground revolutionary movement in Tsarist Russia has dominated our view of the final period of the Romanovs. There is something intrinsically unsatisfactory in this. When we try to write the *history* of modernism as a struggle between the enlightened, progressive, liberal instincts in society locked in a death-grip with the Old Gang, the conservatives, reactionaries, Imperialists and narrow patriots, one can be forgiven for suspecting that not only is

1

ST. PHILIPS COLLEGE LIBRARY

the result a foregone conclusion but that the purpose of the enterprise is to celebrate the glorious revolution of 1914 or thereabouts. Instead of Lenin arriving at the Finland Station, we have T. S. Eliot coming to Church Walk, Kensington, to Ezra Pound's flat. Instead of Father Gapon leading the workers and peasants to the Bloody Sunday massacre, we have T. E. Hulme kicking Wyndham Lewis downstairs at Frith Street. Just about everyone can tell you when Diaghilev took the Ballet Russe to London and when the first Post-Impressionist exhibit opened. The exact date Ezra Pound made his first appearance before the Poets Club is enshrined forever in our hearts. Having made my own contribution to this attitude when I edited an anthology of early criticism of Ezra Pound, it seems more than appropriate to make the point now that such studies have often been misconceived and that we are long overdue a reappraisal of our understanding of the relations between modernists and Edwardians. It is toward that end I propose the following remarks.

What we need to look for are signs of evolution and continuity in the community of artists and intellectuals, for it is within this grouping that imaginative literature holds its greatest sway, and where the possibility of an articulated response to the change in intellectual and social conditions is most available. It is important to get the limits clear, for the history of modernism is not the history of "Edwardian culture." From the point of view of the *whole* culture, there is only one significant tendency that cuts across class lines, and that is the music hall. Samuel Hynes devotes precisely one paragraph to the music hall in his study of *The Edwardian Turn of Mind* (1968); clinging to the title is the dream of a unified and coherent culture, indicated by the irresistible terms—"the Victorian age," "the Edwardian age"—which carry such a meaning. But modernism, at least in its cultural manifestation, has never been anything other than a self-exiled, elitist enterprise. This is precisely the way its characteristic style of allusion works, and its polemics are heavy with overweening assumptions about the availability of certain key literary and historical touchstones. The central opposition between bourgeois and artist is an old one, having reached one kind of expression during the age of Flaubert, Millet and Baudelaire, another during the age of Whistler and Wilde in the 1890s, and a further flowering in the period immediately after the war when "Hugh Selwyn Mauberley," *The Waste Land* and *Ulysses* appeared. 1922, one might say, was made possible by 1914, the date of Wyndham Lewis's *Blast*, the most dramatic and overt message from the modernists to the English bourgeoisie. *Blast* admirably expressed the desire of Lewis, Pound, and the young modernists to provoke, shock and contemptuously insult. It is from this period that we can start to write Pound's biography in terms of his problems with censorship, his struggle with Harriet Monroe's *Poetry* in Chicago, with Harriet Shaw Weaver at *The Egoist*, and with his publisher, Elkin Mathews. In the end Pound gave up on all three. It is a lively story, worth the telling, but not quite sufficiently illuminating on its own. Editors, even of journals as specialized as Harriet Monroe's, and as eccentric as *The Egoist* and Orage's *New Age*, had to keep at least one eye upon the basic fact which determined their existence, the relationship to an anonymous body of readers who were regularly prepared to buy and read the magazine. This is precisely what Pound and the 'men of 1914' declared that they would never do, and it is because we are their heirs that we have accepted their self-justifications, and self-heroization. We have too easily accepted their over-simplifications of the nature of Edwardian taste, and perhaps have been too uncritical of the modernists's intensely partisan view of the past. Between the wars writers of the stature of Dickens and Kipling went into an eclipse for the intellectual community. Not for the bourgeois reading public, clinging to old habits and pieties, but they had ceased to exist for the elite. When Orwell wrote his long, brilliant essay in 1939, he refers to G. K. Chesterton and T.

A. Jackson, a medievalizing Catholic and a Marxist, as the only critics who had shown any recent interest in Dickens; in an obituary note on Kipling in 1936 he wrote that "I worshipped Kipling at thirteen, loathed him at seventeen, enjoyed him at twenty, despised him at twenty-five and now again rather admire him."

We are accustomed to identify all of the liberal and progressive tendencies in Edwardian culture with the effort to persuade the English to become good Europeans. The left-wing is innovative, while the right-wing is mostly narrow-minded, stodgy, and convinced that Newbolt, Noyes and Watson were the major poets of the age. This fundamental opposition of taste often reflected deeper levels of disagreement, different views of the role of poetry in society, and of the nature of poetry itself. The political metaphor, in its conservative variant, was a commonplace of criticism before the First World War. An anonymous review of Ezra Pound's *Personae* in *The Nation* (28 August 1909) gives a striking example:

> ...what these malcontents do not see is that the boundaries of poetic content were long ago extended to such spacious width that it is not humanly possible to extend the *imperium* of poesy, and consequently, that the mode of proper poetic expression is also, within broad limits, practically fixed.[1]

While Browning and Walt Whitman "were rather eccentric, but quite law-abiding citizens," the younger generation, and particularly Ezra Pound, have "mistaken insurgence for strength, treason for originality." When after 1918 the initiative passed to a generation unprepared to listen to this kind of complacency, the political metaphor nevertheless proved useful. The pamphlet which Robert Graves published in 1925, *Contemporary Techniques of Poetry*, was influential in defining the "left" variant, which has survived well into the 1960s in C. K. Stead's *The New Poetic* (1964) and Robert Ross's *The Georgian Revolt* (1965).

The contention between "traditional" poetry and the work of "experimental" writers is not in doubt, but the political metaphor is misleading and anachronistic. For it to be true, or even useful, it would be necessary to believe that the divisions among poets corresponded to a political situation in which the "left" was progressive, innovative, and pro-European, and the "right" was narrowly patriotic—which was certainly not the case. Without discussing the political divisions of Edwardian England in detail, it will perhaps be sufficient to point out that to be European-minded probably meant support for the *Entente* with France, and for that with Russia, both of which were specifically directed towards Wilhelmine Germany. But throughout the "left", not only in the Labour Party but in the radical wing of the governing Liberals, there was considerable suspicion that the dangers of secret treaties, aristocratic alliances, and militarism, would by themselves drag the country into a European war. Leading Liberals had opposed the Boer War, and when they assumed power in 1906 they were reluctant to commit themselves to an active political and military role on the continent. The political metaphor over-simplifies the political situation beyond recognition. At the same time, by lumping all "experimental" writing into a single camp, the category becomes so elastic as to be meaningless. But beneath the specific terms of the political metaphor there is a complex relation of the poet to society in Edwardian England. The right, as the review of Pound in *The Nation* makes clear, were defending a cultural, aesthetic and political *status quo*. To write poetry you had to accept the present limits of that *status quo*. On the left the cause of artistic innovation seemed to lead to other kinds of behavior, sexual and political, which loomed threateningly in the distance. *Vers libre* was thus roughly on a par with the emancipation of women, universal suffrage, free love, socialism and birth control. In a characteristic performance, Eliot swept such considerations aside in "Reflections on Vers Libre" (*The New Statesman*, 3 March 1917):

And as for *vers libre,* we conclude that it is not defined
by absence of pattern or absence of rhyme, for other
verse is without these; that it is not defined by non-
existence of metre, since even the *worst* verse can be
scanned; and we conclude that the division between
Conservative Verse and *vers libre* does not exist, for
there is only good verse, bad verse, and chaos.[2]

Neither Eliot nor Pound would accept such easy
categorization as "left" and "right". The modernism which
they embody is profoundly contradictory: at once revolutionary and reactionary. No simple political metaphor can
possibly be adequate. Its persistence has served to obscure
some of the ways in which modernists and Edwardians were
rather like each other.

Modernists are sometimes said to have a new attitude
towards the traditional cultural heritage. The Victorians,
solemn men with long hair, were relics of the past. But it was
a past which constricted and narrowed, when what was
wanted was something freer, liberating, something solid
without being stuffy. The metaphysicals, the troubadours,
Villon, Dante, the Chinese, and the French Symbolists now
become part of the "tradition." We know from Hugh Kenner and others that these things were not all that new:
Rossetti, and Ford Madox Ford's father, Francis, had done
important work on the Troubadours; Dante was long established as a Victorian favorite; there had been a cult of
Villon in the 1880s; by the late eighteenth century there was
a well-developed taste for *chinoiserie.* Grierson's 1912 edition of Donne culminated a scholarly revival of interest in
the metaphysicals which went as far back as Grosart's Marvell in 1872, E. K. Chambers's Vaughan in 1896, Dobell's
Traherne in 1903 and Waller's Crashaw in 1904.

The modernists' interest in French literature is a case
in point. Until the end of the first World War, when America began to replace France as the predominant cultural
influence upon Britain, the Anglo-French literary relationship thrived. The tone of the eighteen-nineties was that of

the French idiom. In the illustration and design of books, the verse impressionism of Symons and Dowson, and the foppishness of the dandy, Oscar Wilde, the French example was supreme, as it was for the realistic and naturalistic novelists who went to school with Zola. No less important, Englishmen read German and Russian literature in French translation. Writing to George Sturt in 1895, Arnold Bennett named Turgenev, Maupassant, the brothers de Concourt and George Moore as his great masters. "Turgenev," he wrote, "having conceived his story, deliberately strips it of every picturesque inessential, austerely turns aside from any *artfulness,* and seeks to present it in the simplest most straightforward form. That is why he can tell in 60,000 words a history which George Eliot or Thomas Hardy would only have hinted at in 200,000."[3] The English and American expatriate community in Paris, which included at this time Whistler and Sickert, were living examples of the new art for their provincial cousins from Omaha or Oswestry. After the turn of the century, the survivors of the 'tragic generation' of the eighteen-nineties were dispersed and quiescent. Victor Plarr was Librarian to the Royal College of Surgeons. Selwyn Image was Slade Professor of Fine Art at Oxford. Yeats remained in London. Ezra Pound met Olivia Shakespeare, who was Lionel Johnson's first cousin and had been Yeats's lover. She was also the mother of Pound's wife-to-be. Mrs. Shakespeare was widely read in French literature, and occasionally suggested things to Pound. Ernest Rhys, one of Pound's early patrons and the publisher of *The Spirit of Romance,* provided another link with the Francophile eighteen-nineties, as did Pound's publisher, Elkin Mathews, who had published the *Yellow Book* with John Lane, had also published Yeats and many of the poets of the Nineties.

Everywhere you turned in the literary community there was an active knowledge of French, or some other foreign literature. It was an age of translations and popularization: of a somewhat older generation, there was

Constance Garnett, translator of the classic Russian novels, and A. R. Orage, editor of *The New Age* and popularizer of Nietzsche. Ford Madox Ford's wife, Elizabeth Martindale, translated de Maupassant in 1903, to which Ford contributed a brilliant introduction. C. K. Scott Moncrieff translated Proust. T. E. Hulme was the foremost English exponent of Bergson and Worringer. People close to D. H. Lawrence, such as S. S. Koteliansky, translated from the Russian. Richard Aldington made translations from the French and from the classics. In 1911 John Middleton Murry wrote one of the earliest and most acute appreciations of Bergson in English. In 1913 Murry wrote enthusiastically of the classicism of Barrès and Charles Maurras. Murry is given credit for a review of Paul Valéry's *La Jeune Parque* which gave the first full recognition in either England or France of Valéry's achievement. Desmond MacCarthy had read widely in French poetry; after the war he suggested to Edgell Rickword that he write a book on Rimbaud, which duly appeared as *Rimbaud: The Boy and the Poet* in 1924. There were many lesser but conscientious examples of translation, among which might be noticed volumes of German, French and Belgian poetry in the translation of Jethro Bithell, a lecturer in German at the University of Manchester, published between 1909 and 1912. Interest in all things French dramatically increased during the war. F. S. Flint's version of the Belgian poet Emile Verhaeren appeared in 1916. No less prompt to join the bandwagon was Amy Lowell, who published *Six French Poets* in 1915. Maurice Barrès was prominently reviewed in English periodicals. It was like a glimpse of a bygone world when Arthur Symons, now recovered from his mental breakdown and amnesia, published *Colour Studies in Paris* in 1918. Symons' *The Symbolist Movement in Literature* of 1899 proves to be the culmination of one period of British literary Francophilia. The only figure who can be said to rival Symons in this role is F. S. Flint, who has been given much credit as a transmittor of information. Flint's series of arti-

cles on French poetry, beginning with the "French Poetry
Number" of the *Poetry Review* in August 1912, are now
generally accepted as having been the first in England to
convey basic information about post-Symbolist French
poetry. Later that year, the classical anthrolopogist Jane
Ellen Harrison read a paper before the Heretics Society in
Cambridge on Unanimism, in which she generously acknowledged that Flint had introduced her to the subject.
Someone even closer to Pound with an extensive knowledge
of French was Richard Aldington, who contributed reviews
and essays to *The Egoist* and other periodicals which, though
revealing rather little independence of judgment, showed a
good nose for the fashionable taste of the moment. In
addition to his own articles, he turned the literary pages of
The Egoist into a platform for one of Pound's idols, Rémy de
Gourmont. (Aldington edited and translated a two-volume
selection from de Gourmont in 1928, and translated *Lettres
à L' Amazone* in 1931.) All of the advanced literary magazines in this period paid close attention to French literature.
The influence went much further; the prestige of the
Curies in science, and Bergson in philosophy, was formid-
able, to say nothing of the Impressionists, Post-
Impressionists and Cubists then beginning to be known in
London. Society hostesses aspired to create *salons;* senior
artists brought their students together in *ateliers,* all closely
modelled on Parisian practice. It would not seem excessive,
then, to agree with Professor Cyrena Pondrom, who writes
in *The Road from Paris* (1974), that the "...French influence
was ubiquitous in the innovative movements of poetry in
London between 1908 and 1920; French intellectual currents were far more extensive and important than those of
any other foreign origin in this period; and the rhythm,
metric, subject, and form in imagist, vorticist and immediately succeeding poetry all exhibit properties which
were inspired or reinforced by French practices or by
poetry or criticism in the French language." Both Pound
and Eliot entered a milieu in Edwardian England which was

heavily sympathetic towards French literature. It is plausi-
ble that their own interests were shaped by this situation.
The whole of "Edwardian culture" was not aware of or
sympathetic towards French writing, but the educated
bourgeoisie accepted knowledge of France and its culture
as a matter of course. In this the modernists and the Edwardians were at one.

But of course there are discriminations which must be
made among the graceful French ballades of an Austin
Dobson, Belloc's charming essays on French Renaissance
poetry in *Avril* (1904), Maurice Hewlett's *The Life and Death
of Richard Yea-and-Nay,* which contains a vivid portrait of
Bertran de Born; and the day in Paris in 1906 when
Winston Churchill bought the complete works of Maupassant, Balzac, Musset, Voltaire, Lamartine, Chateaubriand,
Madame de Sévigné, *Manon Lescaut* and the correspondence of Marie Antoinette and King Louis, amounting to
some 267 volumes in all. It may have reflected the expectations of an education, or the fact that he was a young M.P.
with no immediate prospect of entering the government.
And then again there is the sneaking suspicion that he had
some shelves to fill. Edward Marsh was said to know Victor
Hugo, Verlaine, La Fontaine and Musset, and could recite
long passages from memory.[4] There were purely scholarly
enthusiasms, like the vacuum-cleaner erudition of a
Saintsbury, and then there was something to the effort
being made by Van Wyck Brooks in America, in an attempt
to locate and lay claim to a "usable past." The conclusions
that were taken from the reading of French poetry were, if
anything, the opposite of those which Brooks retrieved
from the American literature of the Nineteenth Century.
Pound had a clear sense of what was usable in modern
French poetry. "Yet you are right," he wrote to Harriet
Monroe in the Fall of 1913,

> when you say that American knowledge of French
> stops with Hugo. And—dieu le sait—there are few
> enough people on this stupid little island who know

anything beyond Verlaine and Baudelaire—neither of whom is the least use, pedagogically, I mean. They beget imitation and one can learn nothing from them. Whereas Gautier and de Gourmont carry forward the art itself, and the only way one can imitate them is by making more profound your knowledge of the very marrow of art.[5]

For quite different artestic needs, France supplied examples, concepts (such as *symbolisme*), techniques (such as *vers libre*), and slogans (*imagisme, unanimisme*). But French culture could not provide English and American poets with a living relationship with the culture which surrounded them. Modernists turned to tradition, and to other cultures, partly out of a felt inadequacy with their own countries, but also out of a tactical recognition that such things could be used in polemics.

The Edwardian interest in things French was diffuse, and uncritical; but certain figures stand out as exceptions. As an editor, A. R. Orage turned *The New Age* into a great forum for the discussion of contemporary European thought and art, from Marx and Nietzsche to Bergson and Freud. He published frequent articles by young writers on French literature. Pound's "The Approach to Paris" is well-known; perhaps less familiar, but no less interesting, are the articles by Richard Buxton on Henri de Regnier, Jean Moréas, Francis Vielé-Griffin, Stuart Merrill, Francis Jammes, Paul Fort and Albert Samain which appeared in *The New Age* in 1912. Orage himself was not very impressed by "these Frenchmen [who] write of one another gushingly" (apropos a monograph on Baudelaire by Theophile Gautier), but hired as the first major columnist in *The New Age* Arnold Bennett, writing under the pseudonym "Jacob Tonson." Bennett was one of the most discriminating English students of French culture. When a member of the French Academy described Mallarmé as a "fumiste" (that is, a joker, or even a fraud) in the course of a lecture delivered in London, Bennett read him a lesson in the meaning of seriousness in literature. At various points Bennett dismissed the French Academy as "a foolish institution, designed and kept up for the encouragement of mediocrity, correct syntax, and the *status quo*," and described the Théâtre Français as "hopeless, corrupt, feeble, tedious, reactionary, fraudulent, and the laughing-stock of artists." Instead of a blind admiration of all things French, the more discriminating English and American Francophiles picked up in France a convenient way to talk critically about their own society. This is very much what one would expect. France obviously would have quite different kinds of uses for writers who looked across the channel, and there were surprises in store for some. Wilfred Owen wrote home of a meeting with the French satirist Laurent Tailhade in September 1914. Entering the poet's room, Owen found him

> ...at his window in shirtsleeves, mooning. He received me like a lover. To use an expression of the Rev. H. Wigan's, he quite slobbered over me. I know not how many times he squeezed my hand; and, sitting me down on a sofa, pressed my hand against his shoulder.

There is a priceless photograph of Owen and Tailhade from this time. They are standing in a country path. Owen's hair is parted in the middle and carefully plastered down. He is wearing a bow tie, and is standing bowlegged. Tailhade's face is fleshy, alert, middle-aged, self-regarding, standing in a consciously operatic pose, one arm draped around Owen's shoulder. Thus the two cultures meet, both perhaps more aware of the figure they are cutting for the photographer than of each other.

For Pound himself, the story is familiar enough. He has portrayed himself as a student of French "clarity" and "hardness" and in no small measure regarded France as his intellectual and spiritual home. We can distinguish between the early period, roughly from 1906 to 1911 or 1912, when Pound saw Paris through the examples of Symons, Dowson and the eighteen-nineties, when the techniques of impres-

sionism were imported into English verse. The second
phase begins with Pound's violent reaction against the
1890s, and against his own earlier verse, in *Ripostes* (1912).
The complex pattern of influences at work at this time, and
of the evolution of Pound's thought, comes down to
Pound's discovery, with the assistance of Ford Madox Ford,
that the idea that prose, and in particular French prose as
exemplified by Stendhal, Flaubert and Maupassant was
precisely what contemporary poetry needed. From this
perspective, the question of Imagism recedes to the level of
a tactical skirmish compared to the more fundamental and
strategic reorientation implied by the dictum that poetry
must be as well-written as prose. And it is by the formulation
of this *obiter dictum* that Pound learned the use of Gautier
and Laforgue, of a certain flavor of irony and hardness in
verse, which made possible the "Homage to Sextus Propertius" and "Hugh Selwyn Mauberley." There can be no
doubt of the usefulness of the French poets for Pound, but
both Laforgue and Gautier fall into that particular category
of poets which is dominated by Edgar Allan Poe, whose
treatment at the hands of Baudelaire led Aldous Huxley to
write his witty polemic on vulgarity in literature. It seems to
me that "Mauberley" and "Sextus Propertius" (to say nothing of "The Love Song of J. Alfred Prufrock") are incom-
parably superior to anything which Pound may have found
in Gautier or Laforgue. The case of Rémy de Gourmont is
very much of the same kind. Despite the noble efforts of
Professor Glenn Burne, translator and editor of de Gourmont's *Selected Writings* (1966), it seems to me that A. R.
Orage's verdict was essentially the correct one. Pound's
interest in de Gourmont's *Physique de l'Amour* is just one of
those curiousities that turn up increasingly in Pound's intellectual odyssey.

We are left then with a picture of a cultural milieu in
which certain kinds of literary and social assumptions about
the place of French culture were widely shared within the
circles in which the young Pound and Eliot found them-

selves. They did not create that milieu, and there is no
reason to suppose that they made any substantial addition
to its accepted canon. Nor can we any longer follow Kenner,
and the other critics who interpret modernism in calculated
opposition to something called "Edwardian culture" which
they felt impelled to revolutionize and overthrow. Pound
ultimately reacted against the very successes of his own
propaganda, and the growing diffusion of ideas which he
had shared, but which he came to doubt. Pound's opinion of
the young Imagist poets—Flint, Aldington, H. D.—was by
1917 quite sarcastic: they had let loose "dilutions and repetitions." Imagist verse itself had become something marked
by "sloppiness, lack of cohesion, lack of organic centre in
individual poems, rhetoric, a conventional form of language to be found also in classical text-books, and in some
cases a tendency more than slight towards the futurist's
cinematographic fluidity." There is more in this than sour
grapes at "Amygism," for Pound now grasped that "the vers
libre public are probably by now as stone blind to the vocal
or oral properties of a poem as the 'sonnet' public was five
or seven years ago to the actual language..." The first con-
sequence of this insight in Pound's work was the sequence
"Langue d'Oc" which he completed late in 1917, which is
awash in a flood of new-found musicality and archaisms,
and ultimately "Homage to Sextus Propertius" and
"Mauberley." It was not the vacuous Newbolt, or the gallop-
ing rhymes of Alfred Noyes that drove Pound on. What
mattered was a quite distinct constituency of other poets
and sympathetic readers of modern poetry which Pound
had struggled to define and understand throughout that
crucial period between 1912 and 1914 when he was by no
means a principled objector to Edwardian literary life.[6] It
was only when Pound had fully defined the nature of that
elite audience, and his responsibility to it, that he was able to
advance to his own modernity. It was the discovery of modernity *within* Edwardian culture itself which seems such a
remarkable phenomenon: Pound and Eliot were distinctly
part of that culture, they were themselves Edwardians.

William Pratt

Ezra Pound and the Image

The age demanded an image
Of its accelerated grimace,
Something for the modern stage
Not at any rate an Attic grace;

Not, not certainly, the obscure reveries
Of the inward gaze;
Better mendacities
Than the classics in paraphrase!

The "age demanded," chiefly, a mould in plaster,
Made with no loss of time,
A prose kinema, not, not assuredly, alabaster
Or the "sculpture" of rhyme.

Hugh Selwyn Mauberley, Pound's ironic portrait of the artist, stands at the end of the Imagist Decade, from 1910 to 1920, when literature in English became recognizably Modern. These lines from the second section of the poem imply that the modern revolution in literary style came from two main impulses—focus on the image, and defiance of the age, an age which was preoccupied in that second decade of the century with the First World War. Modern literature, it seems fair to say, began as a contradictory art, modern in form, anti-modern in content, and so it was to remain throughout its period of greatness. Virginia Woolf looked back in 1924, in her essay "Mr. Bennett and Mrs. Brown," and concluded that "in or about December, 1910, human character changed." We might not state it so dramatically, more than half a century later, but surely we would agree that literary expression in English—if not human character itself—was radically altered between 1910 and 1920. Probably the best evidence is to be found in the poetry of Yeats, which underwent a visible metamorphosis during that period; whatever personal reasons there may have been for the change in Yeats's style, it brought him all the way from being a Late Romantic, mainly Irish, poet, to being an Early Modern, mainly International, poet in a few short years, justifying the opinion of Pound in 1913 that Yeats was the only older poet writing in English whose work was worth serious study by younger poets.

There is also the fact that most of the poets and writers who would become Yeats's younger contemporaries emerged in that second decade. Pound was as usual a jump ahead in getting into print, though it was not until 1912, with *Ripostes*, that his poetry struck a vein of real modernity. Robert Frost's first books were published in London in 1913 and 1914, and in 1914 *The Egoist* began serializing Joyce's *A Portrait of the Artist as a Young Man*, while introducing such new poets as H. D. and William Carlos Williams and Marianne Moore, and in 1915 *Poetry* magazine in Chicago published both Eliot's "The Love-Song of J. Alfred Prufrock" and Wallace Stevens' "Sunday Morning." When we recall that the first novels and poems of D. H. Lawrence, and the first novels of Virginia Woolf, also appeared in the second decade of the century, we can almost believe that modern literature arose like a phoenix from the ashes of the Great War. But that tempting metaphor is too simple for the process of discovery of a new style that began well before the war and reached its apex in 1922, with the publication of Joyce's *Ulysses* and Eliot's *The Waste Land*. It was a period of mutual inspiration for writers of widely different origins, partly coinciding with the war and being

darkened by it, but it did not have the war as its main subject
or cause. The source of inspiration was mysterious, as always, something Yeats would undoubtedly have called the
Spiritus Mundi, but that might as vaguely be called the Spirit
of the Age, some invisible Zeitgeist impelling very diverse
writers to new forms of expression. It is not scientific to talk
of a Time-Spirit, though so eminent a scientist as Werner
Heisenberg did not blush to take it seriously: he says in his
book, *Physics and Philosophy*, that the Zeitgeist is probably as
much a fact as any fact of science, and that major historic
changes in artistic style are as true a reflection of reality as
major scientific theories, since both are products of the
human mind in its continual effort to express the fundamental nature of things. Ezra Pound in his early critical
writings took a similar view of the equivalence of art and
science:

> The arts, literature, poesy, are a science, just as chemis-
> try is a science. Their subject is man, mankind, and the
> individual.
>
>   ("The Serious Artist," 1913)

Pound maintained that the material of art, human nature, is
a constant, as the material of science, physical nature, is a
constant, but he believed just as firmly in "the art of poetry,
as a living art, an art changing and developing, always the
same at root, never the same in appearance for two decades
in succession" *(Patria Mia*, 1913). Whatever the underlying
causes of Modernism in literature may have been, for
Pound, as instigator, they were rooted in human nature,
which like all organic nature was in continual process of
change, of creation and destruction, birth and death, and
for him, the artist must be constantly striving to "Make it
New," be participating in a perpetual Renaissance.

    Pound, as we know, arrived in London in 1908, with his
first volume of poems in his hand and dreams of a modern
Renaissance in his head. If there were many others of talent
and genius who contributed to the making of modern liter-

ary style, it was Pound who insisted most vehemently that "It is tremendously important that great poetry be written, it makes no jot of difference who writes it," and it was he who did most to encourage, cajole, badger, criticize, and act as literary agent for all the others. Between 1910 and 1920, Pound was at the center of the modern movement, almost, it seemed, *embodying* the Zeitgeist, and it would be hard to dispute Eliot's later judgment that "Mr. Pound is more responsible for the 20th Century revolution in poetry than any other individual" (Introduction to *The Literary Essays of Ezra Pound*). Pound's work as poet, critic, editor, and promoter of the new style was crucial to its initial period, in the decade around the First World War, and what was most essential to his conception of what was truly modern was a single word: Image.

By the time Pound set it down in *Mauberley* that "The age demanded an image," he was ready to bid farewell to London and all that had been accomplished there in the twelve years since he had arrived to seek a new Renaissance. He had launched the Imagists in 1912, and after two years had left them to start the Vorticists; by 1915, he had moved beyond the limited form of the purely Imagist poem which he and H. D. and Aldington and Flint and Hulme had fostered; but he had not deserted the basic principles of Imagism, which were the credo of his Modernism. *Mauberley,* in fact, can be seen as an Imagist poem, built up out of successive concentrated images into a series of portraits of artists and their age—not the pure, static images he had begun with, but contrasting and ironic images that work energetically upon and against each other. *Mauberley* is Pound's pivotal work, looking backward to Imagism and forward to the *Cantos*. It is the same sort of critical self-portrait which Joyce made of Stephen Dedalus and which Eliot made of J. Alfred Prufrock—an autobiographical persona which criticized aspects of the author's own personality, freeing him from certain self-limitations and allowing him to develop beyond them: beyond *Mauberley* are the

Cantos, just as beyond Joyce's *Portrait* is *Ulysses*, and beyond Eliot's "Prufrock" is *The Waste Land*.

But *Mauberley* casts its shadow backward more than forward, containing a capsule history of the Imagist decade, during which Pound had helped to originate a poetic style focused on the image. This image was not all of one kind; it began as a brief, static, spatial, descriptive poem, then became more dynamic as it grew longer, and then more ironic and satirical as the images combined and clashed. One can see this development graphically illustrated in Pound's poetry, starting with the first Imagist poems in *Ripostes* in 1912, then in the relatively pure Chinese images of *Cathay* in 1915 (which in retrospect seem less and less like translations, more like original poems), followed by the satirical images of *Lustra* in 1915, and then the mock-heroic images of *Homage to Sextus Propertius* in 1919 (also more Pound than Propertius as time goes on), and finally in *Hugh Selwyn Mauberley* in 1920. The movement from static to kinetic to ironic images is the main progress of Pound's poetry, the ultimate phase being reached in the first *Cantos* at the end of the decade, where all three types of images are compounded in the Ideogram, Pound's most complex poetic language, a fusion of a number of images into larger wholes, in the manner of Chinese calligraphy (but with groups of word-images replacing the calligrapher's lines). Pound may have portrayed his fictional self, Mauberley, as "out of key with his time," but Pound himself, though at odds with his time, was always in touch even in opposing it, continually confronting the age with images that mirror it critically. *Mauberley* includes, along with its sympathetic and satirical portraits of artists, some of the most telling images of the tragic sense of loss and disillusionment experienced during the First World War:

> There died a myriad,
> And of the best, among them,
> For an old bitch gone in the teeth,
> For a botched civilization,

Charm, smiling at the good mouth,
Quick eyes gone under earth's lid,

For two gross of broken statues,
For a few thousand battered books.

Imagism has too often been scorned or slighted, because as a movement it lasted barely a decade and produced
only a handful of unforgettable poems; but in the work of
Pound it produced a set of poetic ideas more responsible
than any others for the radical changes in English style that
took place from 1910 to 1920, and it produced poems
reflective of a continuing response to the age that was both
creative and critical. Imagism proved in time to be much
more than a passing artistic fad or stylistic novelty, unlike
Dadaism, Futurism, or even Surrealism; for as Stephen
Spender argues in *The Struggle of the Modern*, "The aims of
the imagist movement in poetry provide the archetype of a
modern creative procedure." What Pound and the Imagists
produced was no less than a new definition of poetry,
word-images in natural speech-rhythm, leading to changes
in poetic technique—and in fictional technique as well, for
as Spender rightly suggests, "stream-of-consciousness"
narration is really Imagist prose, the subjective portrayal of
character through selection and association of images in the
mind.

T.E. Hulme must be credited with the initial emphasis
on the image, for he had formed the original School of
Images in London in 1908, the year Pound arrived on the
scene, and he first formulated the doctrine that "Images in
verse are not mere decoration, but the very essence of an
intuitive language" ("Romanticism and Classicism," 1910).
Hulme, with his knowledge of Bergson's philosophy of
Creative Evolution, and his acquaintance with French Symbolism and Impressionism, was the first to reach the conclusion that "the mystery of things is no longer perceived as
action but as impression," and to declare that modern art
"no longer deals with heroic action, it has become definitely

and finally introspective and deals with momentary phases in the poet's mind" ("A Lecture on Modern Poetry," 1910). But Hulme thought of himself as primarily a philosopher, using images as illustrations of ideas, while Pound was always primarily a poet, seeking philosophical justification for his intuitions; and it was Pound who produced the best working definition: "An 'Image' is that which presents an intellectual and emotional complex in an instant of time" ("A Few Don'ts by an Imagist," *Poetry*, March, 1913). It was also Pound who showed in practice how far this definition could be carried into the making of short and then longer poems. Pound emphasized the concentration of intellectual and emotional content possible in a poetic image, though it mirrored only a brief moment of experience. He took the image to be the poet's "primary pigment" and stressed the hardness, or concreteness, of sensory language, telling poets to "Go in fear of abstractions." His primary service to Yeats, as "private secretary" at Stone Cottage in 1913 and 1914, was, in Yeats's own words, to "go over all my work with me to eliminate the abstract," and it was surely Pound who convinced Yeats at that crucial period in his development that "The whole movement in poetry is toward pictures, sensuous images, away from rhetoric, from the abstract" (Yeats, *Uncollected Prose*, p. 414). Besides concreteness, Pound stressed exactness of diction, the *mot juste* of Flaubert, and clarity, and "As regarding rhythm: to compose in the sequence of the musical phrase, not in sequence of the metronome." Thus, along with the image emerged free verse, newly understood as an appropriate organic rhythm, suited to the mood of the individual poem.

Of course, Pound acknowledged in many ways his debt to French writers, in particular Flaubert, his "true Penelope," and Gautier, and Rémy de Gourmont. His favored spelling of *Imagistes* was a gesture of homage to the first school of Modern poets, the *Symbolistes*, whose best-known members were Baudelaire, Mallarmé, Verlaine, and Rimbaud. But Pound criticized the French Symbolists as often as he praised them. The first principle of Imagism was "Direct treatment of the thing," clearly in contrast to Mallarmé's famous dictum that to name a thing was to take away half the pleasure, and whereas Verlaine in his "Art of Poetry" advised an "indefinite music," Pound spoke for "an 'absolute rhythm,' a rhythm, that is in poetry which corresponds exactly to the emotion or shade of emotion to be expressed." Pound wanted the Image to be a more definite and concrete expression than the Symbol, and among French poets it was the "hardness" of Corbière and Laforgue that he praised above the other Symbolists. In speaking of his belief in "absolute rhythm," Pound linked it to "a like belief in a sort of permanent metaphor, which is, as I understand it, 'symbolism' in its profounder sense" ("Vorticism," *Fortnightly Review*, Sept., 1914). In short, Pound's Imagism was intended to carry Symbolism forward towards a greater poetic realism, keeping the poet's vision always in touch with the world of his senses, holding firmly to the principle that truth should be visible *in* things, rather than invisible beyond them.

Pound's definition of the Image is close to the core of the whole Modern movement in literature, which has sought to fuse Symbolism and Realism into an expressive vehicle of numinous perception, where ordinary sensations become imbued with extraordinary and supersensory power. If it has something in common with the Symbol of the French poets, it has even more in common with other key terms which have been invested with meaning by modern English writers. One could draw a direct line from Hopkins' notion of "inscape," as "the soul of art," whereby "searching nature I taste self," which Hopkins found equivalent to Duns Scotus' Latin word, *haeccitas*, or the "thisness" of things, through Joyce's term "epiphany," which he defines in *Stephen Hero* as the revelation of "whatness" of a thing, the expression of a moment when "the soul of the commonest object seems to us radiant," through Pound's Image, to Eliot's "objective correlative," or "a set of objects, a situation, a chain of events which shall be the formula of that particular emotion, such that when the external facts, which must terminate in sensory experience, are given, the emotion is immediately evoked." What all these terms have in common is the belief in Immanence, or Incarnation, the truth revealed through the visible world and expressed in exact, concrete language. Each of these terms has become indispensable to the understanding of modern style, and if Pound's Image has priority over Inscape, Epiphany, or Objective Correlative, it is because it is less specialized, more easily related to poetic language in all ages, but given new significance for the modern age by being made the whole expression; as Pound put it, "The point of Imagisme is that it does not use images *as ornaments*. The image is itself the speech" ("Vorticism," *Fortnightly Review*, Sept., 1914).

Pound's definition of the image was the culmination of a period of prolific experiment which had brought him through many trials and errors to the first crystallization of his own personal poetic style. Pound was the most Protean of modern writers from the beginning to the end of his career, never ceasing to make new experiments in poetic expression; his only real counterparts are in other arts, Picasso in painting, and Stravinsky in music. At first he had imitated a variety of slightly older English contemporaries, the masters of his youth—Browning, Rossetti, Swinburne, the early Yeats—and translated with growing originality from a number of foreign languages, seeking deliberately to enrich English with sounds and images from Provençal, Greek, Anglo-Saxon, Italian, Chinese, French, and German poetry. He was taking his example from the earlier European Renaissance, when writers were using ancient and modern languages to enrich each other, but in Pound's case, it was something like a one-man Renaissance. In his first critical book, *The Spirit of Romance*, published in London in 1910, he began preparing the way for the new style that would emerge in 1912 with the Imagistes. Believing, as

he said in his Preface, that "All ages are contemporaneous,"
Pound defined poetry as an art of precision:

> Poetry is a sort of inspired mathematics, which gives us
> equations, not for abstract figures, triangles, spheres,
> and the like, but equations for the human emotions.

As to what these emotions proceeded from, Pound said in a
later chapter of his book that:

> For our basis in nature, we rest on the indisputable and
> very scientific fact that there are 'in the normal course
> of things,' certain times, a certain sort of moment more
> than another, when a man feels his immortality upon
> him.

Pound then gave a capsule history of Western poetry, in
which he put forward the view that the sense of "immortality" was first translated into the myths of gods appearing in
various forms to men—"speaking aesthetically, the myths
are explications of mood," he said, and the Homeric epics of
the *Iliad* and the *Odyssey* are the classical texts; then, as he
saw it, in the medieval period, under the influence of
Christianity, the myths became metaphors of love, with the
beautiful, unattainable lady of the Provençal and Italian
troubadors becoming an image of transcendent and perfect
love, expressed most fully and satisfactorily in Dante's *Divine Comedy*; the next phase, for Pound, was to be the modern Image. He did not say as much in *The Spirit of Romance*,
but implied it in the criticism that followed in the next few
years, when Imagism was more and more in his mind, and
probably best explained it in describing the process by
which he composed his most famous Imagist poem, "In a
Station of the Metro":

> Three years ago in Paris I got out of a 'metro' train at
> La Concorde, and saw suddenly a beautiful face, and
> then another and another, and then a beautiful child's
> face, and then another beautiful woman, and I tried all
> that day to find words for what this had meant to me,
> and I could not find any words that seemed to me

worthy, or as lovely as that sudden emotion. And that
evening, as I went home along the Rue Raynouard, I
was still trying, and I found, suddenly, the expression.
I do not mean that I found words, but there came an
equation...in little splotches of color.
"Vorticism," *Fortnightly Review*, Sept. 1914

The words were slow in coming; Pound said that he
first wrote a thirty-line poem and destroyed it because it was
a work of "second intensity," and then, six months later,
using the Japanese *haiku*, or nature-image poem, as a
model, he wrote:

The apparition of these faces in the crowd;
Petals on a wet, black bough.

What Pound said he was attempting to make was a verbal
equivalent for a moment of revelation accompanied by
intense emotion: "In a poem of this sort one is trying to
record the precise instant when a thing outward and objective transforms itself, or darts into a thing inward and
subjective" ("Vorticism," *Fortnightly Review*, Sept., 1914).
Consciously or not, Pound's language here echoes the definition of a *sacrament* in the Catechism of the Book of
Common Prayer as "the outward and visible sign of an
inward and spiritual grace." Thus, Pound's description of
the effect of an Imagist poem shows that it was intended to
be an extension of religious symbolism, the modern counterpart of the moment of inspired emotion which had once
produced the lengthier forms of Greek myth and medieval
romance. Of course, the image differs from myth and romance in being instantaneous, without story or sequence,
seemingly independent of time and history. If it succeeds, it
must make up in intensity for what it lacks in duration.
Pound's "Metro" image consists of a single perception of
beauty in the midst of ugliness; what makes it modern is not
so much the city setting as the sense that it happens in a
moment, in the immediate present, now. In defining the
Image in 1913, Pound had said: "It is the presentation of

such a 'complex' instantaneously which gives the sense of sudden liberation; that sense of sudden growth, which we experience in the presence of the greatest works of art."

Not everyone will agree that such an intense emotional effect is possible in a poem as short as "In a Station of the Metro," but one can, by meditating upon it (and meditation, or reflection, is what a short poem demands) certainly see that it contains a potential "equation for the emotions":

$$\frac{faces}{crowd} = \frac{petals}{bough}$$

The faces and petals connote beauty, as the crowd and bough connote ugliness, and the emotion evoked is one of unexpected delight, of human beauty perceived in a sordid city scene. This brief image, with its contrast of light and darkness, foreshadows the constant motif of the *Cantos*, where light and dark images are repeated in so many different forms that they become the equivalents of Heaven and Hell: "In the gloom, the gold gathers the light against it" (Canto XI), or "First came the seen, then thus the palpable/Elysium, though it were in the halls of hell" (Canto LXXXI).

Almost all of Pound's short Imagist poems can be diagrammed in similar fashion, as equations for the emotions. Take, as a further instance, the Chinese image, "Fan-Piece, for her Imperial Lord":

> O fan of white silk,
>   clear as frost on the grass-blade,
> You also are laid aside.

In this equation, or metaphor, the white silk fan is the lady, the hand holding it is her lord, and as the white frost coats the tender grass-blade, so the lord's love for his lady has cooled, and the "fan" has been discarded for another:

$$\frac{fan\ (lady)}{hand\ (lord)} = \frac{grass\text{-}blade}{frost}$$

The emotion implied in this image is that of sorrow in the loss of love, a contrast of warmth and coldness, as the Metro image was a contrast of light and darkness.

From Pound's theory as well as practice of the Imagist poem, it is possible to abstract all of the constants which have become most characteristic of modern style:

1) Instantaneity (of Time)
2) Impersonality (of Viewpoint)
3) Intensity (of Feeling)
4) Irregularity, or Assymetry (of Form)
5) Immanence, or Incarnation (of Truth, Reality, Being)

These qualities, inherent in the simple Imagist poem, were transmitted to the longer and more complex poems of the age, not only the *Cantos*, but *The Waste Land*, *The Bridge*, *Paterson*, and also to the more successful experimental novels, such as *Ulysses*, *Mrs. Dalloway*, *The Sound and the Fury*, which are in essence extended Imagist poems. To the extent that the Imagist poem is a microcosm of the more striking features of modern literary works of much greater length and complexity, it is possible to identify Imagism with Modernism.

It was certainly the image which Pound most looked for in the contemporary writers he admired during the shaping decade of Modernism: he included Joyce's "I Hear an Army" in his anthology, *Des Imagistes*, in 1914, and he praised Yeats for his images, especially "The Magi"; eventually, he helped Eliot edit the manuscript of *The Waste Land* to remove all that was not image. Yeats's favorite among Pound's poems was "The Return," which he commended when he read it aloud at a *Poetry* banquet in Chicago in 1914 as "the most beautiful poem that has been written in the free form, one of the few in which I find a real organic rhythm" (Yeats, *Uncollected Prose*, p. 414). We may take this poem as an excellent example of the development from the static or spatial image to the dynamic or kinetic image. It records a visionary experience, not a sense experience, but Pound maintained from the beginning that an image could be subjective in origin, so long as it was concretely expressed. What distinguishes this poem from the shorter Imagist poems is not merely its length, but the distinctive free-verse rhythm, a musical cadence of the sort which a two or three-line poem cannot exhibit to any notable degree.

THE RETURN

See, they return; ah, see the tentative
Movements, and the slow feet,
The trouble in the pace and the uncertain
Wavering!

See, they return, one, and by one,
With fear, as half-awakened;
As if the snow should hesitate
And murmur in the wind,
    and half turn back;
These were the "Wing'd-with-Awe,"
    Inviolable.

Gods of the wingèd shoe!
With them the silver hounds,
    sniffing the trace of air!

Haie! Haie!
    These were the swift to harry;
These the keen-scented;
These were the souls of blood.

Slow on the leash,
    pallid the leash-men!

This poem may be subjective and visionary in origin, but the image is concrete and dynamic. It depicts the return of the gods to earth, like hunters coming back weary from a chase. Its effectiveness depends upon the coordination of rhythm and imagery, the agreement of the falling trochaic and dactylic feet with the troubled and hesitant motion of the gods and their hounds, returning exhausted, it seems, from the hunt, like ghostly figures in a snowy landscape, yet carrying with them the sense of bravery and prowess, of being "Wing'd-with-Awe" and "Inviolable," virtues still visible even in defeat. The color words "silver" and "pallid" give the image the quality of an etching or line-drawing, a sort of brief Twilight of the Gods sketched in grey and white. What is clear about the poem even at first reading is its fineness of imagery and suavity of music, its elegant visual and verbal harmony, what is indefinite about it is the context of the experience in which the gods have returned: Pound says "See," and invites us to follow his vision, irrespective of when or why it happened to come to him. Much of Pound's poetry does have this kind of obscurity about it, of seeming detached and isolated from time, but this, too, may be seen as the Imagist principle at work: it is the moment of vision or perception crystallized and "liberated" from time, extracted from the flux or continuity of experience which surrounds it. Given the image, out of the poet's experience, we are expected to supply the context out of our own experience. In the case of "The Return," we need not be at a loss for long: the image of heroic defeat is a tragic one, compelling admiration and sympathy, an image of lost grandeur out of the past, recovered momentarily through the poet's evocation, preserving it in memory for all time. Yeats provided his own context for the poem when he printed it, at the end of the preface called "A Packet for Ezra Pound," in his later edition of *A Vision,* where it served as a symbol of the cyclical motions of his gyres of history and human personality. In presenting it, he said: "You will hate these generalities, Ezra, which are themselves, it may be, of the past—the abstract sky—yet you have written 'The Return,' and though you but announce in it some change of style, perhaps, in book and picture it gives me better words than my own" (*A Vision,* 1937, p. 29). Pound himself provided a further context for the poem when he wrote, in one of the very last *Cantos,* near the end of his immensely productive, controversial, and personally tragic life:

The Gods have not returned. "They have never left
us."
     They have not returned.

                                        (Canto 113)

The strength of the poetic image, as Pound conceived it, is
that, being independent of time, it can endure through
time, gathering meaning as it goes, and we may judge from
the example of Pound's work that the very limitations of the
Imagist poem, its isolation and detachment, can become a
strength: the image, because it is free from time, is potentially applicable at any moment of time.

     Pound said early in his career, "It is better to produce
one Image in a lifetime than to produce voluminous
works." What the age demanded was an image plastic,
quick, ephemeral, consumable, like a "prose kinema" or
moving picture; what Pound gave the age were images
brief, quickly taken in, but concentrated and intense, so that
whether they are static, dynamic, or ironic, they persist in
the mind, and at their best endure like solid marble. Imagism is a name for a technique which became distinctively
Modern, and for a belief that, in the rapid motion and flux
of modern existence, it is still possible to experience "moments of immortality," even visionary moments when "the
gods return." Through the immediacy and intensity of a
single image, or a set of images placed together in dynamic
relation, beauty may be revealed as immanent, incarnate,
present now as always. Pound's response to his age was a
criticism of his age, but much of his poetry now seems to
transcend the age he both opposed and expressed; thanks
to his lifelong struggle against the dominant and destruc-
tive materialism of his age, we have, instead of "a mould in
plaster / Made with no loss of time," a large body of poetry
that is "assuredly, alabaster / *And* the 'sculpture' of rhyme."

Peter Makin

Pound's Provence and the Medieval Paideuma: An Essay in Aesthetics

It is generally understood that Pound made of the troubadours' paideuma—their "tangle or complex of in-rooted ideas"[1]—a religion, and of their verse something like a ritual. I think it is not generally understood what kind of religion this was for Pound. An impression is abroad that he connected the troubadours with contemporary heretics, which is correct. There is a further impression that he accepted the general scholarly view that these heretics were ascetics worshipping the Principle of Evil as lord of this world, which is not correct. For Pound, the troubadour cult and the connected heresy were cults of delight and beauty.[2]

Anyone who reads the patches of Pound's Paradise, in the later Cantos, in which pieces of Bernart de Ventadorn appear, will see that this is so.[3] What I want to consider here is not, why did Pound choose to bring what he saw as the troubadour aesthetic, manifested in their verse, into his religion, but, why did he not choose to use the as-it-were given religion of the period, the orthodoxy, as manifested in Christian Latin poetry? And the related question, why should he cook up a new Poundian instant religion at all? It is true that, for example, in the pre-war period, when he was "doing" philosophy in his programmatic way, he took John Scotus Erigena (himself hardly orthodox) into his new

31

tradition. But what he used from Erigena was resplendent light, God as illumination.[4] What he took from the troubadours was (partly) art as ritual; as he himself put it, like the high mass. Why not go to that mediaeval body of culture that contained the aesthetic of divine illumination and ritual expression, the poetry of the orthodox Church?

Perhaps he almost did, perhaps he in fact did. The greatest poet in the Latin lyric of a complex of imagery involving God, the sun, and illuminating wisdom, was St. Ambrose, whom Pound says (in a letter of 1940 discussing Erigena) "I keep on quoting."[5] He had in fact quoted him as far back as 1912, apparently without knowing it. The context is interesting. Pound was considering the troubadour aesthetic, in the very important article "Psychology and Troubadours." He was asking whether one could trace religious feeling in the interstices of the troubadour lyric, whether the relationship between the troubadour and his lady generated some sort of psychic tension leading to the divine vision. "One must consider the temper of the time," he said, and began to quote from Remy de Gourmont's *Latin mystique*. What he quoted first was a piece from St. Ambrose, clearly quite unaware that it was by St. Ambrose and that it was written some seven hundred years before the lyrics of the troubadours he was discussing.[6]

I think it is worth going into this "rendezvous manqué" with Christian Latin. Remy de Gourmont was the go-between. His *Latin mystique* has its own great merits, many of them the merits in Gourmont that Pound was to advertise in his essay of 1920.[7] It is unscholarly but extremely well-read, and I think it is still the best, perhaps the only interesting introduction to the subject. Gourmont never forgets that the monk is a man, with his spleens, his sudden perceptions, his obtusenesses, as in this delicious passage on "the humblest, the least known, the most grieving of monks, Petrus Diaconus, who lived and died at Monte Cassino":

> Perhaps he was a millenarian, but one should take his
> futuritions as pictures of the life going on around his

cloister, the life from which scraps of images, wisps of murmurs reached the cell of man at prayer. In this diatribe against the evil ways of the church and the cloister, two extremely touching lines are inserted at the end of a strophe:

> Ignoravi et nescivi
> Corpus tuum, mulier.[8]

I have remained in ignorance
Of your body, O woman.

Gourmont avoids that pietistic attitude towards religiosity whereby as soon as a work of art is explicitly directed towards a religious subject we cease to analyse it as the product of human states, capable for example of the faults of a bad novel. In particular he endlessly delights in the metaphoric ways of the monks with the Virgin: she is

> the bed of modesty, *thalamus pudoris;* the fountain of sacred sweetness, *sacri fons dulcoris;* the aetherial halo, *jubar aethereum;* the light of the world, *lucerna saeculi;* the royal court, *aula regalis;* the crystal door, *porta chrystallina;* the workshop of the bread of life, *vivi panis officina,* —that is to say that her womb is the bakery where Jesus Christ, the eternal bread, was confected; the battle-tower, through which men entered the celestial city, *turris per quam transit gens...;* the conch-shell full of the celestial dew of grace, *concha roris coelestis gratiae.* [9]

The Virgin's womb is the *Hortus conclusus,* the enclosed garden, where the monks find growing an extraordinary profusion of exotic plants symbolic of the virginal virtues;[10] and this garden is made fertile by a divine mode of operation,

> "by the Dew of pity which itself moistened the stem and fecundated it to bring forth its fruit..."
> Ipse virgam humidavit
> Et in fructum fecundavit
> Ros misericordiae...[11]

—leading of course to the Virgin Birth of Christ. Such metaphorisation, as Gourmont says, became "a cult of the breasts, of the belly, of the womb," which blended easily into theological speculation about the precise orifice by which the breath of the Holy Spirit fecundated the Virgin, and whether she felt any pleasure thereat. All which, as Gourmont by and large concludes, is so much bad poetry, and tends to "destroy the symbol of the Virgin Mother, and suppress half the mystery of the Incarnation..."[12]

    I divagate on this area to show that Gourmont was an adult; that he was not afflicted by the "international Victorian" reduction of all religion to that which could be consumed, and indeed represented, by the blandly-smiling mother and child. But Gourmont did not go into Christian Latin just to toy with other people's sensual aberrations. After his youth he was not a Catholic, but for him as for most of the *symbolistes* the Church was a prime source of emotional material. After pursuing the above peculiarities as far as they go, and repudiating the more ridiculous of them, Gourmont nonetheless defends the explicitness of the mediaeval writers, in favourable contrast to "the timidity of the modern Church, which has had its hymns and proses expurgated by classicising cardinals and doubting literary abbés." The timidity was foolish, he says,

> for, in sum, the whole of Christianity is there, in the conception of Jesus by a Virgin, *sine virile semine*. These simple words, or others like *sine humana connectione, sine virili copula,* etc., suppress the doubt and specify the fact: so the ancient liturgical poets bring them back ceaselessly, as if to proclaim aloud the high absurdity of this mystery, its illogic, its unlikelihood, that is to say its truth, for a sound consideration may conclude that the absurd (if one may thus gloss St. Augustine) is the criterion of true theology.[13]

This perhaps shows that Gourmont was no mere nit-picking rationalist; and his anger against the steady degradation of the Breviary by the authorities since the Council of Trent shows a regard for the quality of the mysteries.[14] What he loves is poetry where the strength of emotion has made the mind alive, "leaping like dolphins" in Pound's phrase, so that the right verbal music and the right image come almost of their own accord. He has that post-Romantic absolutism of aesthetic judgement, that one finds for instance in Verlaine's *Po ètes maudits:* this poet writes "de séduisants vers," that other is "admirable," another has the "génie du rythme." He is quite absolute on the value of music in poetry; Adam of Saint Victor is "le plus magique artisan qui ait fait sonner le psaltérion latin;" and he is probably right not to explain it.[15]

But there is a particular combination of emotional elements which for Gourmont "fait pâlir d'effroi et pleurer de joie esthétique,"[16] "makes one turn pale with terror and weep with aesthetic joy," and that phrase itself suggests what it might be. This combination shows his limits and probably prevented Pound from swallowing him whole. In passages expressing Gourmont's highest appreciation there is frequently a Symbolist languorousness of sweet masochism, peppered with words in *-our-, -eur:*

> Efflorescences suprêmes, la poésie triste et pénitente
> du moyen âge se déploie en deux sombres fleurs amer-
> tumées de cendres, salées de larmes, le *Dies irae* et le
> *Stabat mater,* la peur, la douleur, peur et douleur temp-
> érées par l'adoration, par l'amour.[17]

It is the image of the "bloodied head" of Christ that most calls forth his ecstasy, with the phrase "si douloureusement belle," and it is not surprising that he uses the same phrase a hundred pages later to describe Verlaine's re-creation of the Saviour whose wounds haunt the sinner.[18] The best-constructed parts of *Le Latin mystique* are those which assemble the histories of the *Dies irae,* a hymn to the terror of Christ in Majesty, and the *Stabat mater,* a participation in the suffering of the Mother for her Son.[19] Gourmont may be right to say, as he says elsewhere, that religion is based on "the whole naturalistic poem of the flesh," the rest being a "pretentious and clumsy game for ageing Platonicians;"[20] but if this is so it means that the nature of one's own version of this poem is indicative. Gourmont's poem of religion is very Symbolist. Of course he was a major propagandist for the Symbolists, and *Le Latin mystique* itself is subtitled *Les poètes de l'antiphonaire et la symbolique au moyen âge;* but there were ways in which he had definitely gone beyond the Symbolist aesthetic, ways which are mostly picked out by Pound in the 1920 essay. Had there not been, Pound would not have been interested in him; Pound's essay dismisses the Symbolists casually in one phrase.[21] Nonetheless *Le Latin mystique* has many symbolist virtues and defects. The value of Gourmont for Pound was the cult of emotion, which led to a total shamelessness about it and a fine discrimination unknown to his native America; above all the value was in the knowing that knowledge of these things was private, and attainable only after private effort, and not affected by the fact that the public language of the democratic media was too crude to carry it. Hence Gourmont's arrogance, his exclusiveness, his disdain for the pompous comfortabilities of classicism and all that safely dense culture favoured by the state.[22] Unfortunately Gourmont's Symbolism went as far as the self-justifying exoticism, the Delacroix/Egyptianesque element, perfumes, sweet corruption and sexual sadomasochism, with "Only... mystical literature agrees with our immense fatigue" and the cult of the "obscurs rêves contradictoires qui se donnent rendez-vous en nos âmes éprises de jadis."[23] Hence the cult of jewellery in *Le Latin mystique,* which devotes a separate section in the Index to cataloguing jewel-images, and manages to convert even the *Stabat mater* into a Symbolist bazaar.[24]

Pound would have recoiled from all this stuff. Believing that the divine is in the world though transcending it, that the total organism of the material must be benevolent, he could not accept that divinity or nobility or anything worth having should be reached by denial of normal beauties.[25] When active in London in the nineteen-tens he must have been what a true decadent would have called hopelessly naive. If one may put it thus, he was a very Unitarian Catholic. It was probably the aura of optimism that put Cocteau off Pound's mediaevalism: he probably thought it was the bouncy archaism of a William Morris. One can see the "normality" of Pound in the "Psychology and Troubadours" essay that began this divagation on Gourmont: talking of possible visions attained by the troubadours, he insists that they would have been as it were daylight, Emersonian visions:

> As I have said, our servants of Amor, though they went pale and wept and suffered heat and cold, still came on nothing so apparently morbid as the "dark night."[26]

Having obviously, in his reading of Gourmont's *Latin mystique* if not before, considered the un-Philadelphian possibility that monks might actually reach God by their distortion of the faculties, he dismisses it as not in accord with the "healthy mind in a healthy body."[27] This invokes exactly that bourgeois sanity that Gourmont himself would most have scorned; and is most at odds with the solitary and "supernatural smiles and tears" that Gourmont admired in St. Bernard.[28]

So far I have considered Gourmont as a portal to mediaeval Latin Christianity for Pound, and why Pound chose to leave this portal closed. But there is a foothold for a consideration of Pound's reaction to the Latin itself as distinct from Gourmont's presentation of it, and this foothold is given by the same essay. What after all had made Pound pick out the various pieces of Latin poetry he used in "Psychology and Troubadours," and what made him for the most part later reject their possibilities?

As we have seen, the essay sets up the possibility of a troubadour spirituality based on the tension in the sexual polarity: troubadour reaching towards his lady. He then considers "the temper of the time," quoting as follows:

> Qui pascis inter lilia
> Septus choreis virginum;
> Quocumque pergis virgines
> Sequuntur, atque laudibus
> Post te canentes cursitant,
> Hymnosque dulces personant

He translates in a footnote:

> Who feedest 'mid the lilies,
> Ringed with dancing maidens.
> Where'er Thou runnest, maidens
> Follow, and with praises
> Run behind Thee singing,
> Carolling their sweet hymns.

Then he gives this:

> Nard of Columba flourisheth;
> The little gardens flame with privet;
> Stay the glad maid with flowers,
> Encompass her with apple-boughs.

Pound, following Gourmont, has picked out from the *Iesu corona uirginum* of St. Ambrose and the Mozarabic hymn *De Santa Columba* those parts which most recall, verbally and atmospherically, the *Song of Songs,* and we might pause briefly to consider that poem.[30] It was brought over magnificently into the Latin language by St. Jerome, whose Vulgate was, as Gourmont says, the chief source of language and imagery for all the mystic writers. The *Song of Songs* puts together assemblages of the clear-coloured, the clean-tasting and the firm-feeling of a multiplicity probably not found anywhere else outside Pound's own Canto passages on the lands of his gods and heroes, say the "Seven Lakes Canto" (XLIX), the emergence from hell into the lands of the "founders/ gazing at the mounts of their cities,"[31] or the

> Phoibos, turris eburnea,
>   ivory against cobalt,

> And the boughs cut on the air,
> The leaves cut on the air,
> The hounds on the green slope by the hill,
>   water still black in the shadow.
> In the crisp air,
>   the discontinuous gods.[32]

Pound used the parallelisms of the *Song of Songs,* in the verbal form of the Authorised Version, to make his re-creation of the ancient Hebrew beauty in *Dance Figure: For the Marriage in Cana of Galilee,* which he published only half a year after "Psychology and Troubadours":

> Thine arms are as a young sapling under the bark;
> Thy face as a river with lights...
> As a rillet among the sedge are thy hands upon me;
> Thy fingers a frosted stream.[33]

The Latin of the Vulgate's *Song of Songs* is visible in the *turris eburnea,* "tower of ivory," of Canto XXI, quoted above; the original has:

> Umbilicus tuus crater tornatilis;
>   nunquam indigens poculis.
> Venter tuus sicut acervus tritici,
>   vallatus liliis.
> Duo ubera tua,
>   sicut duo hinnuli gemelli capreae.
> Collum tuum
>   sicut turris eburnea.[34]

The Authorised Version:

> Thy navel is like a round goblet, which wanteth not liquor: thy belly is like an heap of wheat set about with lilies.
> Thy two breasts are like two young roes that are twins.
> Thy neck is as a tower of ivory...[35]

Obviously Pound has used this image for that clear-cut direct sharpness of outline and action that he associates with

the phallic mode of sexuality, and with a clear differentia-
tion of the sexes, though this passage of his Canto is set
about with drunken confusion: the *turris eburnea* for
Phoibos is for the phallic column of the neck and head, such
as we might see it in one of Pisanello's noblemen, or in this
later passage:

> The tower, ivory, the clear sky
> Ivory rigid in sunlight
> And the pale clear of the heaven
> Phoibos of narrow thighs[36]

But the *Song of Songs* is a very purely erotic poem, and it
was probably this unrestrained sensuality that closed it off
as a long-term source for Pound. It would come under the
heading of "normal and eugenic," as Pound described the
sexual function in Catullus's *Collis O Heliconii* and in contemporary Morocco, writing in the "Psychology and
Troubadours."[37] These things he thought of as limited: the
Hellenic/Propertian "Plastic plus immediate satisfaction"
needed some kind of channelling, some delay, some reserv-
ing of the coition for a ritual purpose, such as he thought
"the living conditions of Provence" gave to the troubadour
aesthetic.[38]

The liturgical use of the *Song of Songs* imagery ought to
have given this "necessary restraint." St. Ambrose's hymn,
quoted by Pound, begins

> Iesu corona uirginum,
> quem mater illa concipit,
> quae sola uirgo parturit,
> haec uota clemens accipe...

—which we may translate:

> Jesus, crown of virgins,
> whom that Mother conceived
> who alone was pregnant as a virgin,
> accept these prayers mercifully...[39]

The early Fathers and the mediaeval Church absorbed the

Song of Songs by treating it as an allegory where the Church was the Bride, and the Bridegroom Christ;[40] and so found no difficulty in incorporating its imagery and scenario into hymns to virginity, like this one of Ambrose's which ends with a prayer to ward off "the wounds of corruption," certainly taken to include sensuality.[41] The parts of the hymn that Gourmont selects, and Pound quotes, make a picture of the God rather like that of the Greek hamadryads and nymphs in Zielinski, whom Pound later admired, or the Utopia described in Pound's usury-less future: sweet pastoral groves and meadows where maidens toss flowers and dance.[42] Ambrose's regularity of alternation, broken by quick runs of vowels at line-endings, is the right vehicle for these virgins of the light zone and the "pale foot alternate," straight out of one of the love-rites in the Cantos.[43]

> post te canentes cursitant
> hymnosque dulces personant

And the piece Pound takes from Gourmont on the Mozarabic Liturgy continues this atmosphere:

> Nardus Columbae floruit
> Ligustra flagrant hortuli:
> Fulcite laetam floribus,
> Stipate malis virginem.[44]

If one asks, why could Pound not develop further these elements from the Hebraic paideuma as mediated by the restraining sensibility of the Church Fathers, I think the answer must be that though they may be assimilated as a color into the Cantos, they provide too narrow a base for the development of a modern paideuma. Virgins cannot forever dance in rings; at some point they will be devirginised; Venus, creative and chaotic, had to be faced by Pound, who could not see the Virgin Mother as a sufficiently inclusive solution to "the woman-problem." Sex for him was so primary that it must be harnessed as a force towards transcendence. In 1939 he wrote: "Paganism consisted in a certain attitude toward; a certain understanding of, coitus, which is the mysterium."[45]

For the next piece of Latin that he quoted from Gourmont in "Psychology and Troubadours," Pound made much larger claims:

> As for the *personae* of the Christian cult they are indeed treated as Pagan gods—Apollo with his chorus of Muses, Adonis, the yearly slain, *"Victima paschalis";* yet in the *sequaire* of Godeschalk, a monk in the 11th century, we see a new refinement, an enrichment, I think, of Paganism. The god has at last succeeded in becoming human, and it is not the beauty of the god but the wonderful personality which is the goal of the love and the invocation.[46]

One can see that Pound here wishes to take Christ into the post-Frazerian complex of regenerative ritual, with the *victima paschalis,* the Lamb who is sacrificed at Easter, and to give him a mythology like the Greek—Christ with his virgins like Apollo with his muses. I cannot see exactly what is intended by this "enrichment" in Gottschalk, by which "The god has at least succeeded in becoming human." One can see that in Church Latin Christ is very human, — that the Platonic blank of Augustine has acquired a poetisable life-history, — but, at least after he had read Zielinski, Pound saw the Greek religions also as theanthropic: God and man mediated by god-men. Presumably in 1912 Pound felt that the Greek god-men were beautiful only, and insufficiently human. In Gottschalk, at any rate, Christ has too much of the film-star idea of "personality." I quote from Pound's version of the second sequence quoted by Gourmont:

> Chaste virgins, they immaculately offer unto the Lord the sacrifice of their pure bodies, choosing Christ for their deathless bridegroom...
> Therein Christ sleepeth with them: happy is this sleep, sweet the rest there, wherein true maid is fondled in the embraces of her heavenly spouse...

> It is upon their bosoms that he sleepeth at mid-
> day, placing his head between their virgin breasts...[47]

The method is here become pornographic. Neale is quite
right to worry that the sequence *in nimiam descriptionis
luxuriam hic illic... prorumpat,* specifying the last two verses I
have quoted here.[48] The sequences work by an insistent
denial of the flesh but an equally-insistent manipulation of
its attractions: the emotional charge comes from the virgin
breasts and what is not happening between them and the
head that is reposing on them, and this emotionality is
thought of as spiritual. No thought of copulation is in
Gottschalk's mind, just as no thought of copulation is in the
mind of Lawrence's Miriam mooning through Tennyson
for her Paul; this emotionality is a state, not a means to an
end, but is dependent on sexual elements and is worked for
by Gottschalk obsessively.

Rather like the Church's flirtation with the *Song of
Songs* was its use of the story of Mary Magdalen, which is the
basis of the first Gottschalk sequence quoted by Pound. The
Church was fascinated by the repentant harlot, "whom St.
Francis of Sales proclaimed as the queen of confessing
sinners,"[50] and Gottschalk dilated on the story, with the
Church allegorised as Mary repenting. The sensual contact
was what Gottschalk heightened; this, and the languorous
rhythm,[51] are what distinguish his sequence from a mere
prosaic re-telling, and hence what it is "about."

It is a state of the emotions that Gourmont obviously
delighted in, and Pound also at the time of his quoting
Gottschalk, but it is not something on which Pound could
squarely have built his *paradiso terrestre.* A Malatesta would
have found it adolescent. Hence probably Pound's ditching
of the whole section when he wrote to Eliot in 1940 of "a
1912 note on sequaire of Goddeschalk, etc. The soft sort of
stuff I then did."[52] Between 1912 and 1940 Pound probably
also ditched the "Psychology and Troubadours" argument
about the relation between troubadours and monks, which

definitely takes it that monks reach nearer to God than
troubadours:

> With such the language [i.e. Gottschalk's] of the
> cloisters, would it be surprising that the rebels from it,
> the clerks who did not take orders, should have trans-
> ferred something of the manner, and something of the
> spirit, to the beauty of life as they found it? that souls
> who belonged, not in heaven but, by reason of their
> refinement, in some subtle plaisance, above, yes,
> somewhat above the mortal turmoil, should have cho-
> sen some middle way, something short of grasping at
> the union with the absolute, nor yet that their cult
> should have been extra-marital?[53]

This assumes that those who cry "Lord, Lord," those who
start off with a claim to orthodoxy, have a spiritual advantage over those who do not. I think that Pound was to drop
this assumption, believing that one's vision of the divinity
grew out of one's reaction to the given world, or not at all; in
which sense an unorthodox poet's vision might be just as
religious as a cleric's, and should be analysed and judged on
exactly the same grounds. "The religious man communes
every time his teeth sink into a bread crust," as he wrote in
1940.[54] He also dropped the assumption that the divinity
towards which one must direct one's attention in order to
have a claim to being "religious" must be "the absolute," as
he had called it in 1912; the "Terra Italica" essay of 1931
said:

> The unity of God may be the supreme mystery behind
> the multitudinous appearance of nature. But if you
> put a slab faced boob in the presence of the divine
> unity before he is well out of kindergarten you make it
> extremely unlikely that he will ever understand any-
> thing.[55]

It is possible that Pound later came to value "an orthodoxy,"
but the path thereto was long and difficult, and had to grow
past the juvenility that would accept any kind of ecstasy in a

"God-botherer" as being spiritual.[56]

Gottschalk of Limburg was not the whole of mediaeval Christian Latin poetry, nor even of *Le Latin mystique,* which is full of riches. What happened to the rest, and why did it not "register" on Pound's remarkable sensibility? It could be argued that he would not touch the verse of a St. Bernard of Clairvaux or a St. Thomas Aquinas because he detested everything that they, and the mediaeval Church as a power-structure, stood for. In later essays, especially "Mediaevalism" (1928) and "Terra Italica" (1931/32),[57] Pound sets up an opposition between, on the one hand, the *gioia, dilettanza* of that line of his personal saints from Eleusis onwards, extending through his own adopted mediaevality to the Renaissance, at times underground, at times triumphing, and espousing a reaching towards the fulfillment of all the faculties, a creativity based on belief in the abundance of nature; versus, on the other hand, a reaction from the lack of this faith, an instinct to grab and hoard, to avoid the light because it is too risky. The troubadours are firmly in the former camp, along with Cavalcanti & Co.: this light from Eleusis "set the beauty in the song of Provence and Italy"; it was not a facile hedonism but depended on "some proportion between the fine thing held in the mind, and the inferior thing ready for instant consumption,"[58] whence the place of Sordello and of Bernart de Ventadorn in the Cantos. In the second camp is the Church militant, representative of what Pound's audience would have been accustomed to thinking of as "mediaeval" and what he was at pains to distinguish from his own beloved mediaevality: the Church that flailed its flesh and wallowed in the putrefaction that is to come, and above all (what Pound chiefly detested) persecuted those who could not accept its estimation of worldly values or its map of the celestial topography. To Pound I think it seemed a mixture of fear of one's own innards, expressed vicariously, and fear of any movement not within one's terrified control; which amounted to a lack of faith.

I think one can accept that the element of delight thus described exists in the troubadours. The basis of their aesthetic is in the inseparable conjunction of the well-known "spring opening" and the devotion to the lady. Much wrangling has revolved around the relationship of man to woman in their lyric; this relationship may often seem tedious, obsessive, and masochistic; but I believe that the ratiocination that fills so large a part of the troubadour poetry only takes its meaning from the constellation of images presented so often in the first few lines, which are, as Pound early said, a " 'metaphor by sympathy' for the rest of the poem;"[59] and that in fact most of the songs without a spring-opening or a variant on it are dead, usually not achieving more than a certain cleverness of versification such as one finds in Arnaut's:

> Sols sui qui sai lo sobrafan qe·m sortz

or Bernart's

> Lo tems vai e ven e vire[60]

The true subtlety of sound most often comes when the troubadours get their teeth into their beautiful miniatures of nature evoked in half-a-dozen lines:

> Can l'erba fresch' e·lh folha par
> e la flors boton' el verjan,
> e·l rossinhols autet e clar
> leva sa votz e mou so chan[61]

which may be flatly translated:

> When the fresh grass and the leaves appear,
> and the flower buds on the branch,
> and the high clear nightingale
> lifts its voice and moves its song

For this reason the selection of troubadour elements that goes into the Cantos is not a distortion but a valid reading of their direction.

Can the Church and all its poets be dumped in the

other camp? The essay "Terra Italica" says that the Church emerges from its obscure formative period "riddled with tendencies to fanaticism, with sadistic and masochistic tendencies that are in no way Eleusinian," these tendencies being traceable to the ascetic dualisms like Mithraism that were then strong in the Empire.[62] There is a great proclivity in Pound for the division into devils out of hell and saints, and one sees in his mind's eye an eternal battle the length of history between the underground sect that has its moments of dominance, celebrating the joyous coition of priest and priestess to refertilise the land, and the "police," as he calls the Church authorities when they scatter the bones of heretics: the act of persecution is for him the ultimate sign of perdition.[63] I think that these two currents of history came to be read by him as mutually exclusive:

> We find two forces in history: one that divides, shatters, and kills, and one that contemplates the unity of the mystery.
> "The arrow hath not two points."[64]

And in the same way usury, the grabbing-while-you-can mentality, was deeply incompatible with the creative exploration that produced great art, and an Alexander Hamilton or an Innocent III, the usurer and the persecutor, could do no good, could be associated with no beauty.

It is clear that in the Church of the troubadour period there existed strong tendencies both towards a dualism-based asceticism and towards fanatic persecution. No believer in the dogma that the Principle of Darkness created and rules all material things incontestably, and that we only escape from him in so far as we reach towards death, could have outdone some of the eleventh- and twelfth-century Churchmen in their attempt to create utter disgust for the beauties of this world. No-one of whatever background could have outdone them in their hatred of and arrogant cruelty towards those who disagreed with them. Let us take St. Bernard of Clairvaux, who to many people represents the whole spirit of the twelfth century. He was an immensely influential reformer of Church and monastic orders, a maker of Popes, a theoretician of holy war, the charismatic preacher who made possible the Second Crusade where the Pope had failed, the *Capellanus et Citharista Mariae,* and the writer who perhaps played the greatest part in recalling "devout and loving contemplation to the image of the crucified Christ" and founding "that worship of Our Saviour as the 'Bridegroom of the Soul,' which in the next centuries inspired so much fervid devotion and lyrical sacred poetry," as Butler says.[65] It is with his poetry that we have most to do here. There his rhetoric of disgust is extraordinary. The whole drive of the *Carmen paraeneticum ad Rainaldum* is an absolutely mathematical relationship between punishment of the flesh here below, and elevation towards God.

> Quisquis amat Christum, mundum non diligit istum:
> Sed quasi fetores spernit illius amores,
> Aestimat obscoenum quod mundus credit amoenum
> Et sibi vilescit totum quod in orbe nitescit...

> Whoever loves Christ does not love this world: he despises its loves as foulnesses, considers obscene what the world thinks delightful and finds vile all that shines forth on the earth. He shuns earthly honour as a mortal poison, and having rejected the slime of carnal love longs for the kingdom of heaven with faithful heart already with full faith awaiting the delights of paradise.[66]

We are not called upon simply to turn away from trivialities to higher things; we are asked to participate in a physical disgust as for omnipresent excrement or putrescent flesh, "esca vermium" and "massa pulveris" as this world's vanity is called in the *Rhythmus de Contemptu Mundi.*[67] The Hell awaiting us in the "Hortatory Song" is the fetid fumes breathed by black serpents that we can never escape from, like the Hell in the *Portrait of the Artist* that so struck Pound, and the repeated theme is

> Cur igitur qui sic moritur vult magnificari?[68]

—very like the "O woe, woe,/ People are born and die/ ... /Therefore let us act as if we were dead already" of Pound's Housman parody. The supposed denial of the flesh is a distortion of it, and hence Bernard's curious psychological developments of the theme of Christ's body. The wound in Christ's side becomes the door to Noah's ark for the repenting sinner, whence we exit when the floods of temptation are over, having first sent out an exploratory dove through a metaphorical window.[69] One could say similarly that the famous and influential Sermons on the *Song of Songs* are merely the substitution of a very bad poem for a good one.[70] Bernard attempted personally to fight the divergent religious tendencies in Languedoc with the force of his eloquence, and here we may see his fanaticism. When for example he attacks the heretic Henry, who was said to argue against baptism, such is the ranting incomprehension of his remarks that one cannot even begin to see the basis of Henry's position. Bernard takes his stand on sentimentalism and sadomasochistic guilt[71] and is a worthy forerunner of the Albigensian Crusade, the first Crusade against part of Christendom, that cut off Languedoc in its prime and always retained Pound's condemnation.

When one considers that Bernard disapproved of the splendours of contemporary Church architecture, one might conclude that Pound's case is proven: such a mentality is incompatible with the finer aesthetic distinctions— distinctions between the visible and the sensible—that are the basis of good art. But this line of argument will have to square with Bernard's undeniably excellent poetry. There is the *Laetabundus,* one of the classics that the age expressed its admiration of by shamelessly imitating:

Laetabundus	Joyful
Exsultet fidelis chorus,	let the faithful chorus exult,
Alleluia,	alleluia,

Regem regum	the bed of the chaste one has
Intactae profudit thorus;	brought forth the king of kings,
Res miranda.	a wonderful thing.
Angelus consilii	The Angel of the Council
Natus est de virgine,	is born of the Virgin,
Sol de stella;	Sun from a Star;
Sol occasum nesciens,	a sun knowing no sunset,
Stella semper rutilans,	a star always shining,
Semper clara.	always clear.
Sicut sidus radium	As the star its ray
Profert virgo filium	so the Virgin bears her Son
Pari forma;	equal in beauty;
Neque sidus radio	and neither the star by its ray
Neque mater filio	nor the Mother by her Son
Fit corrupta...[72]	is corrupted...

The simple and spare harmony with which this configuration of light-imagery is put together makes it the equal of any showing-forth of the divine light; its firm ruggedness is of that period which produced the Romanesque nave as a statement of faith. Bernard also has to his name these variations on the *Song of Songs,* as light, as pastoral, and as "ecchoing" as Ambrose's cited earlier, or as Bernart de Ventadorn:

Fons signatus	Sealed fountain
Non turbatus	not disturbed
Bestiarum pedibus,	by the feet of beasts,
Non confusus	not stirred
Sed conclusus	but enclosed
Divinis virtutibus.	with divine virtues.
Exquisitis	with exquisite
Margaritis	pearls
Ornantur monilia...[73]	the necklaces are adorned...

There is the famous, and again very much imitated, "Rosy Sequence" *Jesu dulcis memoria,* where the sounds and the rhythms pant with the lover's longing for Christ.[74] Finally, there is Bernard's magnificent peroration on the transience of this world, and Gourmont brings out the continuity in tone and tradition between it and Villon's three famous ballads:

> Mais ou sont les sainctz apostoles,
> D'aulbes vestuz, d'amiz coeffez...

Bernard's change of rhythm into the remorseless march of the *ubi sunt* in the second stanza here is a mark of genius:

> Qui de morte cogitat, miror quod laetatur:
> Cum sic genus hominum morti deputatur,
> Quo post mortem transeat homo, nesciatur:
> Unde quidem sapiens, ita de se fatur:...
>
> Dic ubi Salomon, olim tam nobilis,
> Vel ubi Samson est, dux invincibilis?
> Vel pulchrior Absalon, vultu mirabilis?
> Vel dulcis Jonathas, multum amabilis?[75]

This statement of the passing of things has something of the strength of Pound's own laments towards the end of his Cantos, or of Bunting in his version of Horace, "You can't grip years." It might disturb a belief that heretic-hunters cannot produce good art.

Can we not then sustain any of Pound's argument? Is the light and exultation of the *Laetabundus* perfectly compatible with the exultant disgust of the other stuff? Should we not be surprised to see one of Pound's later heroes, Anselm of Bec, Archbishop of Canterbury, refiner of a theology of beauty, opening woman up to discover a dung-heap within?[76] Or to find that the Romanesque architecture that Pound admired was the product of a Church so "riddled with tendencies to fanaticism?" Above all, should we reject the drift of Pound's argument that, since the aesthetic of the troubadours was one of delight in the available universe, the culture out of which they grew cannot have expressed itself in the dualist asceticism that is commonly supposed to have been the heresy of Languedoc?[77]

It would be easy to say the Pound is in any case impos-
ing a simple plan on history; and to work out the cultural
reasons why he should want to do so, and thus to dissolve
into the usual circles of relativist anti-aesthetics, subject of
course to the usual smilingly-conceded reserve that someone must work out why the sorter-out of Pound's cultural
predispositions should be culturally predisposed to sort
them into the patterns that have resulted, and so on, *ad
infinitum.* I take this to be the *gran rifiuto,* the preferred
contemporary slick answer. First, I admit it must be accepted that at least with regard to mediaeval history we
cannot discuss aesthetics in relation to personalities, unless
we take personalities as infinitely divisible. As soon as we
start talking about a "Bernard of Clairvaux" as poet, he
disappears in fragments before our eyes. No poetry can
with certitude be ascribed to him, and most of the poetry I
have cited can with certitude be denied him; certainly he
did not write the *Laetabundus,* which was being parodied
before he was born, or the *Jesu dulcis memoria.*[78] Our total
confusion as to who wrote what in these periods is exemplified by the fact that many of our attributions come from
manuscripts of the centuries immediately following St. Bernard, when writers were already becoming unable to distinguish between Bernard of Clairvaux and Bernard of Cluny.
Hymns were compacted into each other, and attributed to
the most famous or "likely" name the scribe could recall,
and these attributions were followed without question by
later pious editors. While it may be of some comfort to know
that the historical Bernard, of whose temper we can to some
degree be certain through his sermons and letters, could
not have written the *Laetabundus,* we are thereby no nearer
knowing what portion of the contemporary religious mind
did produce it.

What Pound does is to posit an aesthetic visible in the
art-form, which he believes to be compatible only with certain ways of life: in the case of the troubadour poetry, the
aesthetic is compatible only with the courageous, fertilizing

religious ethic I have tried to describe; in the case of the Mantegna frescoes, it is compatible only with a non-exploitative economic system. Detecting an aesthetic at a particular period of history, he deduces a way of life there-from; for example, he deduces a ritual from the troubadour lyric, a rite of sexual mimesis. The primary connector is the aesthetic, from which he is prepared to argue quite recklessly, in what any normal historian would call total ignorance, to the way of life of any period. While he does this, and avoids arguing in the reverse directions (from historical "fact" to aesthetic), he is almost infallible, since for him the art-form is an infinitely more sensitive register of aesthetic, sensibility, total attitude to life, than any historical "evidence," which is only filtered anecdotic scrap about "what X did or said." It is probably indicative of his stridency, his need for quick answers, in later years that he starts to argue from historical rather than art-product bases, to say that where there is the historical fact of usury there must be a diabolical way of life, that because Alexander Hamilton promoted high finance he must have been the nastiest American who ever existed.

While he is arguing from aesthetics to way of life, it does not matter that Pound may well attribute such-and-such an aesthetic, or constellated image or ideogram registering an aesthetic, to the wrong historical personage. What matters is to note the existence of an aesthetic and its compatibilities.[79] The usury-Cantos are perfect examples of such complexes of compatibilities and incompatibilities, almost *in vacuo:* it is difficult to relate them realistically to history. The aesthetic complex denoted "Fra Angelico" existed, even if the real author was someone else. It is quite true that the only proof of connection between art-product and way of life is in what oneself has lived or understood, just as it is true that when Pound compared Bruno Walter's conducting to a bust of Mozart carved in sausage, a large proportion of his ultimate readership would simply reject the aesthetic assumptions behind the comparison. Titian, carved in something a little fleshier than sausage, is still regarded as a summit of art. And yet we cannot say "aesthetics are a personal affair"; we go to war for an aesthetic, against an aesthetic; say, British muddle and baggy trousers and tolerance versus Germanic clean limbs, sadism and merciless efficiency, or whatever; all supposed "morals" are based on complexes of images, and one cannot escape, poet or reader, from the attempt to relate complexes of images to lived life, which is why George Oppen was within his rights in calling the usury-Cantos "rhetoric" and its author's politics those of the color magazines.

The statement of a complex of aesthetic interrelations and compatibilities is what an ideogram is, and as Zukofsky has noted, one of Pound's finest is in the essay "Mediaevalism":

> We appear to have lost the radiant world where one thought cuts through another with clean edge, a world of moving energies *'mezzo oscuro rade'*, *'risplende in se perpetuale effecto'*, magnetisms that take form, that are seen, or that border the visible, the matter of Dante's *paradiso*, the glass under water, the form that seems a form seen in a mirror, these realities perceptible to the sense, interacting, *'a lui si tiri'* untouched by the two maladies, the Hebrew disease, the Hindoo disease, fanaticisms and excess that produce Savonarola, asceticisms that produce fakirs, St. Clement of Alexandria, with his prohibition of bathing by women. The envy of dullards who, not having *'intelletto'*, blame the lack of it on innocent muscles. For after asceticism, that is anti-flesh, we get the asceticism that is anti-intelligence, that praises stupidity as 'simplicity', the cult of naïveté... Between those diseases, existed the Mediterranean sanity...[80]

Are these conjunctions legitimate? Would we deduce a religion or a heresy or the impossibility of a heresy from them? First one must define one's heresy, and that not in merely theoretic terms but in terms that can be equivalent to the complexity of the experience that the heresy or religion is, and so must include imagery and sound and all the apparatus of poetry, in comparison with which "prose is NOT education, but the outer courts of the same."[81] We thus come back to aesthetics.

To return then to our original question: what made Pound reject the religious revelation available in orthodox mediaeval poetry, and dig out his own from the troubadours? There was a powerful and beautiful Christian tradition, as I have mentioned, beginning perhaps with St. Ambrose and going right through to the *Laetabundus,* of hymns, especially those for Prime, showing the sun as the light of divine wisdom bringing inspiration:

> Creator of the shining heavens,
> who established the moon as a light in the night,
> and the sun in the courses of the days
> in a fixed path;
> Now black night is driven away,
> the brightness of the world is reborn,
> and a new vigour of the mind
> excites to delightful actions.[82]

There are hymns to the birth of Christ like a sun-god in the solstice.[83] I suppose that Pound could never accept the insistent and overpowering stress on virginity: it excluded that force whose repression we had suffered from ever since the "Greek split." What about the tremendous poetry of the *Stabat mater,* which brings to a conclusion a whole tradition of laments for the bereaved Mother, brilliantly summarised by Gourmont in his book? Pound could appreciate the stiff enduring figure of the peasant Madonna as she is worshipped by the Bretons in Corbière's poem,[84] but only as reportage of a religious state he had no real sympathy with. It would be too close to that exaltation of the "celebrant immolated victims" in Mithraism that he found "the more unpleasant type of present day Christian" admiring.[85] There is a kind of inebriated masochism in it:

Fac me plagis vulnerari,
Cruce fac inebriari
    Et cruore filii;
Flammis ne urar succensus
Per te, virgo, sim defensus
    In die iudicii.[86]

Cause me to be stricken with wounds,
to be made drunken with the Cross
and with the blood of the Son;
lest I be burned up with flames
let me be defended by you, O Virgin,
on the day of Judgement.

The terrific and remorseless *Dies irae*, likewise the late flowering of a long mediaeval tradition, uses the Crucifixion as a counter in a bargaining of pity against guilt between sinner and *Iustus iudex ultionis*, "just Judge of vengeance."[87] Pound finally responded to this kind of thing with the "European good sense" of this song:

Pere eternel vous avez tort	Eternal Father, you are wrong
Et ben devetz avoir vergogne,	and really must be ashamed,
Vestre fils bien amis est mort	your well-loved son is dead
Et vous dormez comme un ivrogne.[88]	and you are sleeping like a drunk.

Pound thus dismissed a millenium of religious myth on the grounds of an aesthetic distaste. I think one can call him an aesthetic Protestant, but an historical Catholic. He believed that one should personally choose from among the past states achieved by man, but by aesthetic means rather like those behind his kind of "comparative literature." He did not believe, on the other hand, that one should revise the tradition in one particular direction on the basis of an historical rationalism, for example that the Old Testament, or the life of Jesus, "came first."[89] In what sense, Eliot queried from his safe orthodoxy, did Pound believe in the gods thus chosen? But in what sense did Eliot believe? His own orthodoxy seems so much a rational choice, a careful selection from among possible race-pasts. Pound's aesthetic basis for belief seems as valid as any, and if it seems to rule out the Catholic sense of the need for a continuity of the group's special cultural heritage, even that may be changed by his worry in 1959 about "the distinction between A Church, an orthodoxy, and a collection of intelligent obser-vations by individual theologians, however brilliant."[90]

Out of mediaeval religious verse, though not this time in Latin, there is at least one element that Pound received more favorably: the aesthetic of St. Francis of Assisi. Pound offered his own version of the *Cantico del sole* with enthusi-asm in *The Spirit of Romance;* in it, he says,

> that "little sheep of God" speaks to the glory of the Father Eternal in a free, unrhymed verse with a rhythm strong as the words and well accompanying them:

> Most high Lord,
> Yours are the praises,
> The glory and the honors,
> And to you alone must be accorded
> All graciousness; and no man there is
> Who is worthy to name you.
> Be praisèd, O God, and be exalted,
> My Lord, of all creatures,
> And in especial of the most high Sun
> Which is your creature, O Lord, that makes clear
> The day and illumines it,
> Whence by its fairness and its splendor
> It is become thy face;
> And of the white moon...[91]

Pound's version has its own stiff, ecstatic strength, and he was pleased enough with it to offer it again in the *Confucius to Cummings* anthology half a century later.[92] Twenty-eight years after *The Spirit of Romance,* the *Cantico del sole* has honourable mention in connection with two prayers Pound has found in Italian schoolbooks, wherein the "Mediterranean moderation" is apparent:

> *We implore, omnipotent God, thy clemency, so that thou having made to cease the flooding rain, shalt show to us through the calm sky the hilarity of thy face. In the name of Jesus Christ our Saviour. So be it.*
>
> Hilarity. The italian is just that: *l'ilarità del Tuo Volto.*
> These seem to me to belong rather to the universal religion of all men, than to any sect or fad of religion.[93]

Obviously Pound brings out the qualities in St. Francis that attract him when he speaks of the "hilarity" of God's face. St. Francis trod the very delicate line of poverty as a hygiene of the faculties, staying this side of asceticism — the distinction that Pound tried to make clear when he spoke of poverty, not misery, as holy.[94] St. Francis himself was a great poet, and the few authentic sources concerning him show him to have been concerned for a worthy adoration of God in physical, artistic terms.[95] It is clear from the surviving early writings that his great fear of buildings and of books for his own followers was a fear of institutionalization, not of the trap of physical beauty;[96] he regarded the Church, with which he was obliged to have close dealings, as something that could not but threaten the pursuit of spiritual aims, but which remained absolutely necessary to men and to himself in that only through it could the rite be performed.[97] He had no absolutist idea that men of pure spirit could address themselves directly to a God of pure spirit. Since St. Francis is so pre-eminently the poet of God visible in His creatures, despite the mocking irony of modern commentators it is neither a great surprise nor a betrayal to see his seed flower into that great surge of building and painting at Assisi and elsewhere that leads into the early Renaissance; the Renaissance which itself, Raffaello Morghen has argued, was more a product of the whole Franciscan movement of any supposed exhumation of the late Greek rationalism and anthropocentrism.[98] Morghen describes the "classic" spirit of the twelfth century, the age of St. Bernard of Clairvaux, as the ideal of the Christian conquest of the world by force of arms and legislation, the ideal of the "soldier of Christ" in unrelenting struggle against heretic and unbeliever by Inquisition and by Crusade. He shows how the Dominicans, the second great mendicant Order in the flowering of the Franciscan age, continued this essentially mediaeval tradition: taking their origins from the necessities of their fight against heresy, they based their preaching on the defence of orthodoxy and the recall to the crudest mediaeval asceticism, threatening the sinner with imminent and inexorable Judgement. With the Franciscans of the thirteenth and fourteenth centuries there was an essential "difference of tone." Following St. Francis's "precise and enthusiastic perception of the beauty conferred on the universe by God," the "freedom from earthly bonds in his surge of love towards God and His creatures" represented by the legend of his marriage with Lady Poverty, and the example of his attempt to convert the heathen by force of love not arms, the Franciscans based their effort on more benign emotions. With an awareness of human weakness, they tried to move their audiences towards renewal by love, not fear. They instituted "Mounts of Pity," peoples' banks like the ones that figure in the Cantos of Pound; campaigned against the cruelties of usury; and labored for the public good. The apotheosis of St. Francis came only half a century after his death, in the great new churches of Assisi, Florence and San Giminiano which are the first flowerings of the early Renaissance, and where Giotto, Simone Martini, Cimabue and others conspire to make these new architectural forms the home of a splendour of sunlight and color. Morghen argues that the essence of Franciscanism was a religious attitude that "recognized in the values of the spirit the highest expression of human dignity," and that this was at the same time the most essential basis of the Renaissance. The Renaissance was not, as is so often held, a revival of rationalism out of antiquity

via Aquinas's Aristotelianism, which only became a dominant influence after the Catholic Counter-Reformation.
The thirteenth and fourteenth centuries were the age of the
Franciscan theologians, like Duns Scotus and St. Bonaventure, whose faith was a voluntarism, an "opposition to that
pre-eminence of the intellectual faculties over the will"
which was the basic principle of Thomist Aristotelianism.

If this historical thesis is valid, it makes Pound's love for
Fra Angelico, for St. Francis and for the troubadours less of
an aesthetic eclecticism and more of an historical necessity.
It is pleasant to find history concurring with aesthetics. St.
Francis, according to this view, is the clear precursor of
those elements in the Renaissance that Pound favoured; for
Pound was never chiefly interested in the mere scholarly
digging of the Italian literati, and his lists of great painters
will be found to have more of the religious revelation about
them than the mere Greek study of muscle. One can see the
troubadours as in some degree St. Francis's precursors: the
revealers of the vision of light in nature and in woman,
whose culture, cut off short by the Albigensian Crusade,
nonetheless passed on its discovery to the early thirteenth-
century North Italian culture in which St. Francis and Sordello were contemporaries. This was the current of
mediaeval spirituality that Pound was able to use. It expressed itself in the vernaculars of Languedoc and of Italy;
the other, perhaps more "classic" and orthodox current of
spirituality, that of St. Bernard, Innocent III and Thomas
Aquinas, wrote its poetry in mediaeval Latin, and it was this
Latin poetry that Pound rejected.

Donald Monk

How to Misread: Pound's Use of Translation

so far as I can see only two, possibly, are admitted, by
him, to be his betters—Confucius, & Dante. Which
assumption, that there are intelligent men whom he
can outtalk, is beautiful because it destroys historical
time...

Charles Olson, Mayan Letters, 5

Early on in his disillusionment with the shift from
Imagism to Amygism, during his propaganda work for
Vorticism, Pound was to insist

> The Image is not an idea. It is a radiant node or cluster;
> it is what I can, and must perforce, call a VORTEX,
> from which, and through which, and into which, ideas
> are constantly rushing.[1]

When I first read this, years ago, I must confess to thinking
it arrant nonsense. How could the Image, shaped as words
already, and words as close to mosaic and sculpture as
possible, also have some unidentified energizing force at
loose on the page? Wasn't this fuss about Vorticism, as
Wyndham Lewis suspected, Pound looking for the easiest
and fastest way out of the implicitly inhibiting, static, self-
limiting duration of the single image? Particularly so since
at this time Pound was using *Blast,* the revolutionary organ

of the movement, to publish such manifest low-tension *chinoiserie* as the "Epitaph" on Li Po:

> And Li Po also died drunk.
> He tried to embrace a moon
> In the Yellow River.

where it is difficult to detect the rushing of any ideas at all. I jumped to the conclusion that the real way out of Pound's impasse was, *via* Fenollosa, into the ideogram—that juxtaposition of images where the agility of the linked minds of author and reader is accountable for whatever drive and motion is generated in the poem. Pound, locked in a dead-end aesthetic that could only handle the single-unit poem, was amusing himself playing with ideas he gave no real emotional assent to, so that the VORTEX was perhaps entirely a device to shock the bourgoisie, a mere gesture in the direction of modernism.

But this is to forget to take into account a very early definition indeed of a similar process in poetry, to be found in the series of essays "I gather the Limbs of Osiris," Pound's most stimulating early theoretical thought, published in *The New Age* from 7 December 1911 to 15 February 1912. Out of a context dealing with the difficulty of the practising poet in translating and/or learning the modes of foreign traditions, and the cultural necessity of knowledge best reached in this way, we find this:

> Let us imagine that words are like great hollow cones of steel of different dullness and acuteness; I say great because I want them not too easy to move; they must be of different sizes. Let us imagine them charged with a force like electricity, or, rather, radiating a force from their apexes—some radiating, some sucking in. We must have a greater variety of activity than with electricity—not merely positive and negative; but let us say $+$, $-$, $\times$, $\div$, $+a$, $-a$, $\times a$, $\div a$, etc. Some of these kinds of force neutralise each other, some augment; but the only way any two cones can be got to act without waste is for them to be so placed that their apexes and a

line of surface meet exactly. When this conjunction
occurs let us say their force is not added one's to the
other's, but multiplied the one's by the other's; thus
three or four words in exact juxtaposition are capable
of radiating a very high potentiality; mind you, the
juxtaposition of their vertices must be exact and the
angles or 'signs' of discharge must augment and not
neutralise each other. This peculiar energy which fills
the cones is the power of tradition, of centuries of race
consciousness, of agreement, of association; and the
control of it is the 'Technique of Content,' which nothing short of genius understands.[2]

Ignoring for the moment the question-begging involved in
the phrase "technique of content" and discounting altogether the vague egotism in "genius," we have the first
Vorticist theory, much superior to the programmatic and
condensed "futuristic" version of 1914/16. It is superior
because it does not take as its starting-point the "Image"
(posited as that is on another, later, dubious aesthetic) but
what is unarguably the material of poetry, *words,* which is
seen as possessing its own inherent life and energy from
"the power of tradition, of centuries of race consciousness,
of agreement, of association." In effect, it is a contextual
theory; any word will have its own enrichments from its
place in the history of the language, and will reach back in
its derivation from its roots into other languages. The ex-
pertise of the individual poet will align words to release
their optimum potential, reinforcing by his own context the
multiple and associative context the words' history implies.
In translation, we may guess, the very languages themselves
will be made to lay their contexts alongside each other. This
doubled drive, of experimentor and translator, reaches
back into the past and releases the energy of the past into
new forms. It accounts for what Pound ruefully phrased in
1927:

I have been accused of wishing to provide "a portable
substitute for the British Museum," which I would do,
like a shot, were it possible. It isn't.[3]

You may have experienced a strong sense of *déjà en-tendu* in all this, or so I would hope. For it is in essence (dealing with words as opposed to the accomplished ar-tifact) the theory behind that cornerstone of modern criti-cism, "Tradition and the Individual Talent," which postu-lates western literature as a live, metamorphosing museum, "portable" insofar as memory, response and association can make it so. More and more over the years Eliot's essay of 1919 reveals itself not as unassailable critical dicta but as an apologia for the poem that was becoming, with Pound's intercession, *The Waste Land.* Hidden in the labyrinth Pos-sum was to make of impersonality and the objective cor-relative is the controlling question of what kind of con-sciousness gets into a poem and what is to control it. Pound, long before his friend and colleague, long before a tech-nique of his own could substantiate his theory, had crystal-lized the same question. His answers assume a life in lan-guage itself, a life that poets of each generation must redis-cover, develop and invent, a life necessarily beyond the poet's own personality, reaching back into the history of his language, into its constituent elements and hence to the very culture he inhabits. Finding a language for Pound could also be a cultural odyssey, *vide* the *Cantos.* Granted his starting points, it *had* to be.

So that for Pound, even at the time of his involvement with Imagism, translation was a very complex task indeed. For convenience, the issues may be compressed thus: cul-turally, to make available to an ignorant public the richness of his own area of specialization, Provençal verse; critically, in his exploration of Provence to present it as a watershed in European poetry (taking Arnaut Daniel as its greatest mas-ter, to establish the central transition running Sappho-Catullus-Propertius-Ovid, Daniel and the troubadors, Cavalcanti-Dante); creatively, to incorporate into his own metric, his "voice," his very way of thinking, the special sound of Provence. The first major complication I would like to point out is that this committed Pound to a forward-looking quest for a new language (free of pre-Raphaelite encumbrances, clear as was the "prose tradition" that Imagism embraced), an exploration of the Latin roots that underlie both Provençal language and thought (the main corridor, or perhaps more aptly, elevator-shaft, travelling vertically to the significant past), and, impossibly complicating the issue, grafting onto his own and his culture's language and idiom a sound alien to it. The difficulties mushroomed when Pound chose to decide that poetry naturally divided into three *genera*—melopoeia, phanopoeia, and logopoeia—which meant including a Chinese tradition of the visual image and a subtlety of word-play begun by Propertius, briefly emergent in Heine, then back in full force, 1900 years or so from its beginning, in Laforgue.

Let us for the moment concentrate on the difficulties implicit in Pound's believing, as he did in 1913, that

> any study of European poetry is unsound if it does not commence with a study of that art in Provence.[4]

The fullest ascription of the source of the beauties of Provençal is to be found in 1920, where Pound makes a comparison with the complexities of Arabian music:

> In especial one notes the "extraordinary" length of the rhythm pattern units, comparable to the medieval rhyme-scheme of Provençal canzos, where for example, one finds a rhyme-pattern which begins its six-ply repeat after the seventeenth different terminal sound. In this Arabian music, as in the Provençal metrical schemes, the effect of the subtler repetitions only becomes apparent in the third or fourth strophe, and then culminates in the fifth or sixth, as a sort of horizontal instead of perpendicular chord. One might call it a "sort of" counterpoint; if one can conceive a counterpoint which plays not against a sound newly struck, but against the residuum and residua of sounds which hang in the auditory memory.[5]

Starting from analysis of the brilliance of Daniel's technique (the poem instanced is his "L'Aura amara") Pound rapidly

passes to the deeper implications of "horizontal counterpoint" as the nature of one kind of music in poetry. How far
the subtlety of this concept can be pushed is evident in
Eliot's postulation of the "auditory imagination" and the
creation of the music in *Four Quartets,* where complex, non-
sonic rhythm (the sound of meaning) may well be supposed
to hang in the air from one poem to the next. More immediately to our purpose is that this kind of sound simply
did not translate from Provençal. In defining "melopoeia"
Pound observes:

> It is practically impossible to transfer it from one lan-
> guage to another, save perhaps by divine accident, and
> for half a line at a time.[6]

And this recognition comes when he has restricted
"melopoeia" to meaning words "charged, over and above
their plain meaning, with some musical property,"[7] retreat-
ing from the deeper and surer account of *melos,* defined in
1911 as being "the union of words, rhythm, and music (i.e.,
that part of music which we do not perceive as rhythm)."[8] So
chronic is the difficulty presented that it surely accounts for
Daniel's work being put before us by Pound in the equivalent of a double-text (*Instigations,* 1920) where the reader
must be supposed to develop a rudimentary working
knowledge of Provençal (sounds and pronunciation, obviously, but maybe also seeing its intermediary status between
Latin and modern French). Frost's belief that "poetry is
what gets lost in the translation" could seem to be winning
out over Pound's position. Even so, all was not loss. Some of
the Provençal sound could be taken into English direct—its
system of measure

> (a) by number of syllables, (b) by number of stressed
> syllables, which has become the convention of most
> European poetry[9]

—which was singled out, along with quantity in Greek verse,
alliteration in Anglo-Saxon, assonantal terminations in
Spanish, as the tradition's major innovatory contribution to

world-literature. Pound the explorer-experimentalist saw that it was

> not beyond the pales of possibility that English verse of the future will be a sort of orchestration taking account of all these systems.[10]

Grandiose as the intention might be, something of the kind must be acknowledged working in the *Cantos,* while the cross-grafting on to an Anglo-Saxon alliterative base of quantity, syllabics, and assonance in all its forms shows itself in the major work of Hardy, Owen, Auden, Bunting and Hughes—the English experimentalists of the century.

Turning from the technical, there is an equally important dimension of how Pound came to the past, also covered in "I gather the Limbs of Osiris," where he says:

> We know in reading, let us say, de Born, what part is personal, what part is technical, how good it is in manner, how good in matter.[11]

Conjoined to the word "matter" (are there echoes here of the "technique of content"?) and the fact that de Born's stormy life was one point of attraction, the oddness of the linking to the "technical" should make us prick our ears. For no fewer than four poems (five, if we count the enigmatic "Provincia Deserta") dealing with de Born have survived the vicissitudes of Poundian reprints. I refer to the two translations, "Planh for the Young English King" and "Na Audiart," the imitative recreation "Sestina: Altaforte," and the uncategorizable "Near Perigord." The "matter" of de Born to which Pound refers opens up wide areas of liberties taken with the past, for none of the five poems limits itself to translation. "Na Audiart" and its later manifestation "Dompna pois de me no 'us cal'" are put before us as examples of how "to make 'Una dompna soiseubuda' a borrowed lady or as the Italians translated it 'Una donna ideale'." Though we see in the second version Pound trusting more to straight translation rather than vague, pre-Raphaelite approximation, it is the "matter" that truly in-

volves Pound. How de Born developed a particularly rare
type of poem of compliment and, beyond this, how this
relates to idealizing love poetry such as Cavalcanti's "Donna
mi prega" and Dante's use of Beatrice as the center of *La
Divina Commedia* make us look through the poem into the
tradition, as if it were a translucency. "Planh for the Young
English King" offers us yet another dimension: it stands
before us as something more than a formal, courtly expression of grief, but, as Pound is to ask elsewhere, is the "something more" personal loss or de Born dealing in a subtle
game of politics with the Plantagenets, maneuvering the old
king by reference to his dead son? The historical context
that could clarify this is lost for ever, so that history itself
becomes an ambiguity. "Sestina: Altaforte." is Browningesque, self-attestedly a digging up of the past "Eccovi! Judge
ye! Have I dug him up again?" But even here, alongside all
the swagger and rambunctiousness, there is a reach beyond
the method of Browning (if not his diction) in that the form
into which the poem is cast is one with which de Born
himself experimented. Not only is the man's "personality"
given us, but the forms he would have used to express it.
Nevertheless it is the enigma of de Born the man, poet-
lover-strategist, as opposed to the greater skill of, say, Arnaut Daniel, to which Pound is attracted. A few years later
Yeats was to lament the death of Robert Gregory, saying he
was "Our Sidney and our perfect man." Sidney, another
poet-lover-strategist, is familiar to us from a closer history,
and perhaps a more romanticized view of chivalry. De
Born's imperfections—his war-mongering, his duplicity,
the lack of smoothness in his verse technique—are what
appeal to Pound. For they mirror the imperfections of the
age de Born lived in, the imperfect knowledge any person
has of any other, and the sketchiness of our knowledge of
that age—crumbled away, it may be, just as the remnants of
Sappho's work have, dramatized by Pound in "Papyrus" in
the same period.

Casting around for a solution to the enigma of de Born

and his relationship to his age Pound invented the form of "Near Perigord." Hardly a translation, it is nevertheless totally dependent on our seeing how Pound approaches Provençal. In one aspect it shows him investigating the de Born poems he had translated in the light of his own experience of the countryside of Provence, as exemplified in "Provincia Deserta." In another it is a dramatization of the processes by which the past atrophies and conceals itself. On either count the notion of the vortex, images in motion, ideas pouring into, through, and out of images is central. Since the poem is self-confessedly a look at the impenetrability of the past—it begins with an exhortation to "read between the lines"; its second section turns away even from these ambiguities, beginning "End fact. Try fiction"; and the whole concludes with the kaleidoscopic manifold "a broken bundle of mirrors" it may be that it was so composed as never to yield one knowable meaning. But, moving as it does between polyglot quotation and adaptation, its dynamism self-evidently depends on our seeing the past in some several aspects, or, more accurately, Pound's own mind generating different modes of force around these aspects. There are at least six different modes: untranslated original(s), translation, paraphrase, allusion to other translation, collation in translation, and translatorese—the entire spectrum of Pound's experimentation with opening up the past.

Looking more closely at these various modes we encounter even further complications. The three direct quotations all reverberate beyond what they say. The epigraph ("A Perigord, pres del muralh / Tan que i puosch' om gitar ab malh") gives us words of de Born's that lock, Provence against Italian, with Dante's ("Ed eran due in uno, ed uno in due") epigraph to the third section in a quick scan of Romance word-formation that is readily understood (with the exception of "malh" = "mace") and possibly shows the drift to the smoother, more supple, more modern Italian as an actual, inevitable historical process that made de Born, like his language, anachronistic. And the severance of these quotations from their true contexts loads them with ambiguities in their new location. Are we to refer back to the de Born original and find it continues with him defiantly riding up to Perigord's walls on a charger; or, taking the words as they stand, are we to read the warlike propensities of the man and his age in the fact that distance was judged by how far a mace might be thrown? And the words of Dante, in the original damning de Born in Hell to carry his head like a lantern because in his life his heart and his head were used to stir up strife, are susceptible as they now stand to being read as meaning a split between emotion and intellect (just such as Eliot's "dissociation of sensibility") or the two can be seen as de Born and Maent themselves, fatally two-in-one as are Paolo and Francesca in another classic episode. The third quotation (I take the reference to "trobar clus" as included within it), Foix's "Et albirar ab lor bordon" ("And sing not all they have in mind") refers simply, as it stands, to "concealed" singing, the special art of Provence. In the original there is again a reference to violence (be armed when you meet the French, they don't say plainly what they mean), obliquely and ambiguously commented on when we have seen that Foix' territory was "a neat ledge," unlike de Born's "one huge back half-covered up with pine." Were violence and slyness endemic to the times? Whatever else, Pound shows us in these twisting meanings much the same as the troubadors, withholding or doubling their implications, made in *trobar clus*.

If this interlarding of three contexts alone does build up the kind of complexity I have indicated, then to cover the interaction with the other five modes would be impossibly lengthy and complex at this juncture. So I would like merely to point to certain aspects and sketch in what look like the key ramifications. In the compressed translation of Dante's picture of de Born from the *Inferno,* what is intended by the transfer of the original's *terza rima* into Pound's pet hate, blank verse? When de Born's paraphrase

of de Born's "Dopmna pois" is compressed into four lines
(*ll.* 6–9) plus *ll.* 69–75 (even freer in their handling of the
original) why does the *envoi* of that poem appear for the
first time? (If to give a greater sense of immediacy, with its
direct address to the jongleur, Papiols, it still leaves us with
the problem of why Pound hedges round the explicit sexuality de Born puts into the original, first dealt with by Pound
as "never a flaw was there/Where thy torse and limbs are
met," and afterwards entirely softened into a Cavalcanti-
like praise of pure love). What are we to do when we find
that the marvellous poem in miniature of the lines "Pawn
your castles, lords!/Let the Jews pay" comes from Pound
having grafted on to "Baro, metetz en gatge" an anti-
Semitism disseminated in general through de Born's work?
As for translatorese, clearly the mode of the poem's third
section, we may say this represents Pound giving up hope of
adequately rendering a lost truth. But does this adequately
explain that the poem is at this stage in a composite pre-
Raphaelite idiom that mingles "day's cycs" (a modern form
of the Anglo-Saxon kenning) with the archaic French of
"émail"?

Overall we may say the poem conforms to a mimetic
line, not of the past, but of Pound responding to the past,
finally making an inadequate language mirror how the past
grows dim and eludes us. So that the *real* ways of encounter-
ing the past—through translation, through getting first-
hand knowledge of Provençal, through challenging the
simpler notions of interpretative analysis—are dramatized
on the page before us, and, furthermore, provide a crucial
vortex into all of Pound's treatment of the past. The key to
the poem is not in de Born's psychology, whatever we make
it out to be, but in our seeing Pound's psychology at work in
response to "dead" personalities whose communication is
now in a "dead" language. The solidarity of the past that
Pound drives down into, from the rock-hardness of the
"originals" through to the deliberate insubstantiality of his
own "imagining," is of varying degrees of trustworthiness to

build on. The kind of verbal strengths and activities that the
poem gives us show in their respective reliabilities *how* we
should approach the past. Only the originals, we find, can
be trusted—ambiguous as they may be. Rather more than
being a "portable museum," the poem is a vortex of ener-
gies of different kind; rather more than being an elevator
down to the "floors" of the past, as in a museum, the poem is
a "rock-drill" testing the solidities of what makes up our
response to the past.

It is not the obvious kinds of ignorance of Provençal
that we should look at, nor even what that ignorance betrays
(as when Pound mistranslates, in the "Planh," "en mort" (in
death) as "Sir Death," thus giving us "Romance" in its sen-
timental rather than semantic and musical aspect). For he is
experimenting also with his own change of sentiment, over
the years of his experience in translation. Significantly, the
poem makes no attempt at the intricate six-ply music of
Arnaut Daniel, the special glory of Provence: de Born, its
subject, is a ruder technician altogether (Daniel is seen
within the poem conjecturally "deploring his technique")
and when Daniel speaks *in propria persona* in the poem it is in
a realistic, cut-and-thrust vein with the warrior-poet-king,
Richard Coeur de Lion. There is a reach towards Provençal
"melopoeia" only in the distorted paraphrases from de
Born. In the main the poem finds what music it possesses
not in sound, but in the associative collation of different
languages (of all kinds—one (in especial) being invented for
the purposes of this poem and never used again), looking
for its "horizontal counterpoint" this way, and its colloca-
tion of sharp images. The most immediately satisfying parts
of the poem are its images—Perigord's road network
"spread like the fingertips of one frail hand," "the ar-
mourer's torch-flare/melting on steel," or

>   Richard goes out next day
>   And gets a quarrel-bolt shot through his vizard,
>   Pardons the bowman, dies

with its debts to the impressionistic novel-technique of Ford

Madox Ford, and the patent self-projection of Pound into de Born ("a red straggling beard" of a man whose "green cat's eye lifts toward Montaignac"), where Pound surely insists "I am in this poem. I *am* this poem." And so, since "melopoeia" doesn't translate, why not look for its equivalent in images, even in images left in their original forms and languages? It is unhelpful to quarrel with Pound on the level of local mistranslation. The method itself makes much more radical departures from what is commonly accepted.

For what Pound finds in this pre-Renaissance world is very much what he wants to find, and insists on our sharing. Some Arnaut Daniel he couldn't adequately translate (he makes four attempts at the treasured, "total" image "En fetz escut de son bel mantel endi" between 1910 and 1920, and fails to get it into one, single line, even). Similarly, with "E quel remir contral lum de la lampa," he has to resort to the ridiculously loose word "glamour." No matter: the phrase itself "e quel remir" will appear in the *Cantos,* and (Pound by now having decided, as "Tradition and the Individual Talent presupposes, we can be expected to read *all* the work of a major author) the particular reverberations, sensual, melodic, ideal, should transmit to us. So also should Cavalcanti's "dove sta memoria," the nub, for Pound, not only of "Donna mi prega," but of this entire tradition of holding the past because of what is loved in the past. There are intrinsic difficulties in all languages, perhaps insuperable: in his essay on Cavalcanti (1910–31), Pound translates "Donna mi prega" as "Because a lady asks me," in the magnificent translation of the same poem in Canto 36 as "A lady asks me": cause-and-effect are not the only problems—the word "donna" itself, unless given in the vocative, simply doesn't translate insofar as the notions of personal male possession and generic female attraction can be fused in medieval Italian. Part of what is needed is the notion of "womankind" (Canto 79), as instanced in Nicoletti's admiring exclamation, watching a cat balance on the top bar of a railing, of the thrice repeated "La Donna" in Canto 74. If words as basic as this cannot cross the frontiers of language, perhaps Pound's own alternatives were better: to establish a direct quote as leitmotif, and to take as his own the basic effect of what attracted him. The history of culture itself perhaps demanded this. When Marlowe uses Ovid's line "Lente, lente, currite noctis equi" he could assume that a sixteenth century audience would be familiar enough with the original to find a special thrill in the change of context from amorous to terrified delay: in a twentieth century context, fragmented in its roots, the use of a Latin or Provençal or Italian quotation is in effect an unironic imperative to *discover* what the original is and what tradition it represents: the irony is in the record of culture itself, not in the reference to it. In addition to this Pound can be seen in the process of culling effects that seem specially memorable to him from out of the past: Arnaut's "contral la lum de la lampa" is an effect clearly close to what Pound translates from Propertius as "the honey-coloured light," or what Golding translates from Ovid as

> A redness mixt with whyght upon her tender body
>   cam,
> As when a scarlet curtaine streyned against a playstred
>   wall
> Doothe cast like shadow

Both in rhythm and in image Pound is a relentless borrower.

Whether Pound was making the past his own, or being gobbled by the past, is debatable. But he certainly allowed himself great latitude in his approach to translation proper, *vide* his assertion that all authors use up to "say 4% blanks ...for the timing, the movement etc."[12] or that many adjectives in Homer have "only melodic value."[13] On this basis, what are we to make of *melos*? Above all Pound was to continue to insist on the primacy of "content," as in

> The quality of translations declined in measure as the translators ceased to be absorbed in the subject matter of their original.[14]

Just so—but where is the perimeter of subject matter, say, when Pound approaches Provence? At his most succinct Pound lists the aims of good translation as being

1. Real speech *in* the English version
2. Fidelity to the original
   a. meaning
   b. atmosphere[15]

where it is impossible not to think that for him "meaning" and "atmosphere" have become co-substantial. It is this kind of thinking that allowed him to render the folk-wisdom of the Chinese *Odes* in a negro-minstrel dialect.

But this lapse of decorum should not blind us to Pound's conviction that the past was alive, that the materials of poetry were unchanging, that the primary task was to "make it new." Accordingly he is prepared to grant the highest of places to his fellowtranslators of the past. For him, Golding's *Metamorphoses* "form possibly the most beautiful book in the language"[16] which indicates a very wide notion of native tradition indeed, where the sheer weight and relevance of Ovid's work, sympathetically recorded and rendered by Golding, make it a sixteenth century classic. If this kind of invasion is seemingly extreme, what are we to make of a tradition of translation, including Marlowe for his *Amores,* not his drama, where it can be said:

> After Chaucer we have Gavin Douglas's *Eneados,* better
> than the original, as Douglas had heard the sea.[17]

except that it makes Yeats' approach to the "myth-kitty" look positively tame? We may grant of the tradition that Pound so extols (Chaucer, Golding, Douglas, Marlowe) that

> in each of which books a great poet has compensated,
> by his own skill, any loss in transition; a new beauty has
> in each case been created.[18]

We may even grant that certain forms, ideas, achievement, are more integral to the "tradition" than others. But trans-

lation superior to the original? And yet hadn't there been
the example of what Baudelaire made of Poe? But what
Pound is essentially driving at is that there is through the
ages *one* true tradition, always breaking into life again,
sometimes in development, sometimes in translation of a
major order. We are supposed to believe that when Pound
translated the *Seafarer*, not only did he make the past newly
available, but in the act of translation confirmed that this
particular part of the past was genuinely and permanently
valid. Translation, in part, defines the tradition. The *Seafarer*, seen as the high point of the Anglo-Saxon tradition,
would be expected to reach, however far away, the verse
craftsman who was finding what alliteration could do; so,
accounting for certain tones in Arnaut Daniel's verse

> it is as like as not he knew Arabic music, and perhaps
> had heard, if he understood not the meaning, some
> song in rough Saxon letters.[19]

But it would be inaccurate to say that Pound believes only in
the endless ramifications of influence. For translation to be
able to surpass its original source there has to be a con-
tinuum of both form and matter—the poetic principle
itself—which the translator has more adequately expressed.
The principle of Anglo-Saxon verse, if it possesses the
uniqueness that Pound believes, must also be universally
valid. Inevitably:

> I once got a man to start translating the *Seafarer* into
> Chinese. It came out almost directly into Chinese
> verse, with two solid ideograms in each half-line.[20]

To pick Pound up on the local mistranslation (say, Anglo-
Saxon "laene" for "laen," "transitory" for "loan") is to strain
at gnats.

On *Cathay* (1915), and Pound's acknowledged reputa-
tion as "the inventor of Chinese poetry for our time," I have
little new to add. Here again he uncovers a tradition, dependent on its special conventions, and brings to life poetry
within that tradition—notably that of Rihaku, or Li Po. I

take him to be correct when he says, giving one reason for his success with this phanopoeic tradition:

> Phanopoeia can, on the other hand, be translated almost, or wholly intact. When it is good enough, it is practically impossible for the translator to destroy it save by very crass bungling, and the neglect of perfectly well-known and formulative rules.[21]

Of its nature the image MUST translate more immediately than melody. Whether or not the Chinese ideograph functions as Pound, following Fenellosa, believes, I am not competent to judge: but from this time Pound tried to incorporate in his work the virtues of this tradition, which focuses on the primacy of noun and verb in nature, in effect, almost, finding the verbal action *in* nouns and working away from the odious copula "is." Though this was a natural continuation for an Imagist, it is still disconcerting to find the poet who had spent so much time trying to catch the melopoeia of the Romance languages confessing,

> When I did *Cathay*, I had no inkling of the techniques of sound, which I am now convinced *must* exist or have existed in Chinese poetry.[22]

This admission was as late as 1937, and is only slightly mitigated by the statement of three years later:

> When it comes to the question of transmitting from the East to the West, a great part of the Chinese sound is no use at all. We don't hear parts of it, and much of the rest is a hiss or a mumble.[23]

Pound may be correct in deciding that the phonic values simply cannot be brought over from Chinese into English, but it is odd in the extreme that the matter never received his attention. It shows very clearly that by 1915 the three divisions of poetry were mutually exclusive, and that the "technique of content" may very well exclude the notion of the aesthetic whole and be closer to something paraphrasable than one would like to see. The subject matter was undoubtedly congenial to 1915 (though the dates seem to

argue against a current trend to make *Cathay* a war-poem).
What is remarkable is that in translating conventional,
fixed-mode poetry Pound was to find his own style,
highly-patterned yet supple *vers libre,* while finding a language and syntax that at least in some degree best renders
Chinese. Manifestly the *ethos* of the original reaches
through Pound and becomes assimilated into an English
tradition, in some measure making good, by example, what
he claims for the excellence of Gavin Douglas and Golding
as translators.

What I would like to concentrate on is the most celebrated of Pound's howlers in mistranslation. This occurs,
you will recall, when, misled by Fenellosa's annotation,
Pound runs two poems together and makes a new composite poem, Rihaku's *River Song.* Exacerbating the difficulty,
the two poems are quite distinct in character: the first being
a hedonistic *carpe diem* happily accepting that ephemera
constitute the heart of all things, while the second is a
sycophantic plea for the poet to be given court employment.
They are difficult enough to accept as the work of the same
personality, let alone collate into one artifact.

Some very unexpected, revealing, and "experimental"
results spring from this unwitting juxtaposition. The *River
Song* proper ends

> (If glory could last for ever
> Then the waters of Han would flow northward.)

Almost in the troubador mode Rihaku embodies a disdain
for *vanitas mundi* by objectifying his feelings within the
immediate landscape (the unalterable fact that all the rivers
of China flow south and east). Because of the unemphatic
tone, Pound missed that this was in fact a concluding note,
and, when confronted with the title of the poem following,
proceeded to translate it as a "bridge-passage," if you will,
into the sycophancy of the second poem. The four lines of
the title emerge thus:

> And I have moped in the Emperor's garden, awaiting
> > an order-to-write!
> I looked at the dragon-pond, with its willow-coloured
> > water
> Just reflecting the sky's tinge,
> And heard the five-score nightingales aimlessly
> > singing.

Divergences from the original there are in plenty. "Orioles" are turned into the more plangent "nightingales"; the word "aimlessly" appears out of nowhere; while "moped" also has little textual justification. One can see what has been subtly added to the continuing visual felicity. Pound, sensing a radical change of mood, takes the sycophantic self-abasement Rihaku is expressing and transforms it into a cynical *ennui*, shrugging its shoulders at the empty forms insisted on by court life. From the simple link "And I have moped..." (Pound is excessively fond of lines beginning "And" in his Chinese work: *Exile's Letter* begins 30 out of its 74 lines this way) the world-weary resignation fed into "And" operates much like Vonnegut's "So it goes." It is in fact an omnipresent tone in his presentation of Rihaku. And this ironic tone colours everything presented in the composite-poem from this juncture. Sycophancy is turned into a mask of conformity. Wryly, the Emperor's supposed lack of aesthetic response is caught in the two lines:

> The Emperor in his jewelled car goes out to inspect his
> > flowers,
> He goes out to Hori, to look at the wing-flapping
> > storks...

where the artificiality of the "translatorese" mirrors the imperial pretentiousness—"wing-flapping" showing a mechanical response to the natural, and the ponderously inflated "inspect" (for the basic "see" in the original) pomp-and-circumstantially shows the birds being looked at in the same way as the guards. It is a non-language of bureaucratic blockheadedness that produces the barbarism in the "unre-cognised" title of the "second" poem, "order-to-write." This sententious language, co-existent with a deliberately lengthened, invertebrate line cannot be Rihaku. But it does serve as a bridge from hedonism to contempt of excessive formalism. Significantly, in its rhythm and ironically-inflated tone it is the accent of the *Homage to Sextus Propertius*.

Having reached the heart of this essay—the distinctive sound and movement of Pound's verse, the shape he cuts into time—I would like to make one last detour, but a detour that goes back to the basic structure of this paper. It is a commonplace that Pound's division of poetry into three categories—melopoeia, phanopoeia, and logopoeia—is an unfortunate compartmentalization, since the best poetry is at the same time melodic, visually realized, and marked by an active play of the intelligence. What is not so often remarked is that this tri-partite division corresponds exactly to the order of Pound's successive enthusiasms as a trans-lator and definer of the true tradition—Provençal, Chinese, then Latin (where Propertius is taken along with Catullus and, to a lesser degree, Ovid as representing a lively, sensual mode that specifically excludes Virgil and Horace, the clas-sics of earlier times). So that the self-evident evasiveness of what "logopoeia" consists of ("the dance of the intellect among words") must be seen in the light of Pound's finding the last and most subtle component in world-literature, where there will be a clear intention to assimilate that note to his own work. As we would expect of a poet already in full mastery of his own style, there are indications of a readiness to be very free indeed with the original (even if we accept that "logopoeia" is necessarily much more a matter of tone than paraphrasable content).

In his comments on the nature of "logopoeia" for the translator Pound grants himself a very wide latitude:

> *Logopoeia* does not translate; though the attitude of

> mind it expresses may pass through a paraphrase. Or
> one might say, you can *not* translate it "locally," but
> having determined the original author's state of mind,
> you may or may not be able to find a derivative or an
> equivalent.[24]

He is looking at an "attitude" or "state" of mind as his
material, and cutting totally loose from any idea of "local"
translation. *Propertius*, then, is already firmly a matter of
atmosphere, not fact. Two wide-reaching divergences from
the normal modes permitted translators should be mentioned in this context. In 1932 Pound wrote to John Drummond:

> I wonder how far the *Mauberley* is merely a trans-
> lation of the *Homage to S.P.*, for such as couldn't un-
> derstand the latter?
> An endeavour to communicate with a block-
> headed epoch.[25]

which suggests, against all the odds of the radically differ-
ing styles of the two poems, that their material and meaning
are coterminous. Substantiation of this strange fact, which
implies, surely, that the *Propertius* is made over into Pound,
can found in the letter to Thomas Hardy, which says:

> The Propertius is confused—the Mauberley is thin—
> one tries to comfort oneself with the argument that the
> qualities are inherent in the subject matter.[26]

Indeed a grave disservice has been done in extolling the
virtues of *Mauberley* (which *is* "thin," however brilliant an
Englishization of Gautier it may be) over those of *Propertius*,
with its wider range of tone, more consistent point-of-view,
and more adventurous metric. Part of the trouble, no
doubt, is our difficulty in making out what the "subject" of
Propertius is—whether Hardy was right in saying that an
overtly Browningesque title such as "Propertius Sol-
iloquises" would have guarded it against the attacks on the
eccentricities of it if seen as a translation proper. It seems

that a second aspect of the intention in the poem is worth insisting on:

> If possible I shd. even have wished to render a composite character, including something of Ovid, and making the portrayed figure not only Propertius but inclusive of the spirit of the young man of the Augustan age, hating rhetoric and undeceived by imperial hogwash.[27]

This clearly takes the poem into its real dimensions as a translation of "atmosphere" rather than "meaning," and, *pace*, the difficulties involved in the notion of "intention" (which is a crucial point in Pound's translation), does seem to have happened, in that the note of Ovidian ribaldry is omnipresent in the poem. And it seems a more adequate description of what we actually encounter in the poem than the better-known formulation that the poem consists of

> the super-position (?), the doubling of me and Propertius, England today, and Rome under Augustus.[28]

which smacks of being a *post facto* rationalization in response to the attacks of the establishment.

Donald Davie, in his invaluable little book in the Fontana series of Modern Masters, has done a great deal towards letting us see *Propertius* for what it is. On the technical side he makes three points of prime importance: (1) the special sound of the poem comes from the employment of dactylotrochaic rather than iambic rhythms (*i.e.* Propertius' quantitative metre has been utilized in Pound's fight against the dreaded pentameter); (2) that the poem is consciously written in non-language, *babu* English, the sadly pretentious use of elaborate vocabulary and syntax of subject nations aping their masters (so that the multiple awkwardnesses in the poem, where Pound drifts into translatorese or unassimilable structures, are *functional*, a large part of the poem's "meaning"); and (3) that these deliberate incongruities do not inhibit a real range of feeling, or limit it to the comic (*i.e.* leave open the chances of modulation into "profound and plangent feeling... with a mastery that is the peculiar glory of this poem," so that the uncertainty with language becomes a *dramatic* mode). Davie sums up the matter brilliantly:

> Thus it appears that by wholly transposing "imperialism" into language, into the texture of style, by forgetting his own existence "for the sake of the lines," Pound has effected a far more wounding and penetrative critique of imperialism in general than he could have done by fabricating consciously a schematic correspondence between himself and Propertius, the Roman Empire and the British.[29]

His argument seems to me unassailable, and has the great merit of making us steer clear of the difficulties of the "intentional fallacy," and deal only with the "achieved intention," the poem. Moreover, it takes the classic indictment of Pound being "a sensibility without a mind" and makes the adaptability of his consciousness the virtue it ought to be accepted as.

For in poetry it is consciousness that generates energy, and *Homage to Sextus Propertius* is Pound's response to Propertius, no more and no less. The poem is a vortex, the two "charged," "aligned" cones being Pound, the reader, the translator, the poet, and the other the Latin of Propertius. So of necessity we have a poem "from which, and through which, and into which, ideas are constantly rushing," since in addition to the doubling of Pound and Propertius there is the reader with his own response to these likenesses and unlikenesses. A possible source for the deliberate licence, as opposed to earlier translating liberties, of *Propertius* could be the second chapter, "Forgetting of Foreign Words," of Freud's *Psychopathology of Everyday Life,* first published in English in 1914. Interestingly enough, the main matter in this chapter is an exercise in finding dirty meanings in a line from Pound's bugbear, Virgil. The line should read "Exoriare aliquis nostris ex ossibus ultor" but a mental block by Freud's subject drops the word "aliquis," and the familiar

Freudian tactic reveals that the inner censor has been at work, obliterating the word because of associations with female liquidity embarrassing to the subject at the time. The two words associated, "aliquis" and "liquor," are, incidentally, words that Pound deliberately botches in *Propertius* in terms of straight translation. What happens to the Virgil lines is a kind of obverse counterpart to *Propertius,* where the game may well seem to be reading in as many dirty meanings—*consciously*—in the act of response to the text. The most famous example of this is the translation of "tacta puella" as "devirginated young ladies," where the overtones in "virgo intacta,' may or may not have been in Propertius' mind. But the backing-up of this by the translation of "intacta...Arabia" as "virgin Arabia," which takes the platitude of the bureaucratic mind and insists on the pre-eminence of sexuality (because the *context* has thrust "devirginated" into our minds), surely gives us a sex-ridden *ambience*. But, reading Catullus, isn't this how the Rome of the times appears? And Propertius himself, who insists "My genius is no more than a girl," the girl in question being a known prostitute, isn't he, whether an ironic poet or otherwise, obsessed by sex? As a sign of the times is this kind of "spread" of meaning more or less acceptable than the concentration that asks who put the "cunt" in "Scunthorpe"?

This is not the only, or even the dominant, kind of word-play the poem offers. Indeed, the "bending" of language occurs on a massive scale, and normally in such a way as makes us more aware of the nature of our language. To translate what should be the "extensions" of Empire as "distensions" is not only to point out the immorality of imperialism but the nature of our word-formations using Latin prefixes on Latin root-words. To take "orgia" and render it as "orgies" rather than "mysteries" is indeed to point to the deterioration of religious activities in Rome, but it also indicates how language itself is in a process of movement. And to render "Cimbrorumque minas" as "Welsh mines" may be geographically as well as semantically incorrect, but it does show that imperialism knows no natural boundaries and also that the scale of levies involved reach into national natural resources. When Pound decided that "logopoeia" did not translate locally, that decision meant, inevitably, that his word-play would reach to its only circumference—his own consciousness. What may not be in Propertius, is nevertheless in Pound's response to Propertius, so that the poem gives both an approximation of the original and the process by which Pound arrived at it. Consequently we have a marvellous density of texture, as in the gorgeous nonsense made of "Tale facis carmen, docta testudine quale" ("such music upon his well-skilled lyre") in

> Like a trained and performing tortoise
> I would make verse in your fashion, if she should
>   command it

It is incredible enough that a "howler" on this scale should ever have been seen as ignorant mistranslation, but why wasn't the nonsense of the "tortoise-versifier" followed back to the root, "testudo," (with its two branches, "lyre" and "tortoise") to show the bizarreness of the Latin itself (or of the material for musical instruments!), thus to see that the verbal comedy acts out for us the unavoidable barriers between live and dead languages, which in fact can be turned to advantage, as a new source of poetic energy?

Juxtaposition is at the heart of "logopoeia," just as much as of "ideogram." And as Davie observes, comedy can modulate to the plangent. In

> And if she plays with me with her shirt off,
> We shall construct many Iliads

there is irony in putting the flatly prosaic "shirt" against the (non-figuratively) epic "Iliads." But, for *this* Propertius, as maybe for the historical, Cynthia is equivalent to epic matter: and to catch the multiplicity of this European verse lineage, we are given a subtle superimposition of a iambic sound just forcing itself from the base dactylotrochaic metre. The metre is alive, just as is the language. Section X

gives us a world of debauchery and revelry, where the
drunken Propertius is hustled into Cynthia's presence by a
bunch of sexually precocious youngsters, that may not be
Rome, but is an acceptable equivalent. Cynthia, magnificently garbed in "a new Sidonian night cap" (the strange-
ness of the language catches the idiosyncracy of the fashion), exclaims disdainfully: "You are a very early inspector
of mistresses." Propertius' discomfiture is perfectly caught
in his garbled *babu,* but it might be pointed out that this
comes from the playing-off of words imported from different stages of development of Latin languages (Fr. "Mait-
resse," L. "spect" root of many aspects of seeing). Crestfal-
len, Propertius has to admit:

> There were upon the bed no signs of a voluptuous
>   encounter,
> No signs of a second incumbent

What we respond to here is the construction in parallel ("no
signs of") which mimics Latin syntax and reinforces the
Latin roots of "incumbent" and "voluptuous," not as linguistic trickery alone, but also as the defensive cloaking, in
neutralized words, of a sexual jealousy Propertius, only too
well aware of the actualized sensualities involved, daren't let
himself think too precisely about. The Johnsonian portent-
ousness is censoring out the physical in about the same way
that Freud's subject lost the word "aliquis" altogether.

  Propertius derives its energy from the juxtaposition of
Pound's mind and the original text. In its own way it includes as much vandalism towards the past as
resuscitation—the inlay of foreign vocabulary and metre on
a supposed norm. And this free-and-easy approach not
only to translation, but the nature of language itself—
contempt for the iambic norm in order to find a more
organic pulse, organization by syntax, glorification of
nonEnglish—is not quite a unique phenomenon. It is what
we find in Whitman. Pound, usually a man positive to the
point of dogmatism, expresses contradictory feelings to-

wards Whitman throughout his life, but his description of himself in 1909 gives us a very recognisable image of the poet of *Homage to Sextus Propertius:*

> Mentally I am a Walt Whitman who has learned to wear a collar and a dress shirt (although at times inimical to both)[30]

"Me imperturbe," "sounding a barbaric yawp," but oriented to the past rather than the future—this is the Pound of *Propertius*. T.S. Eliot to the contrary (whose dismissal of the presence of Whitman's influence on Pound should be measured by his cool review of *Propertius* and responsibility, as Faber editor, for its exclusion from the most easily available selections of Pound), Whitman's base rhythm is noticeably something that Pound converts to his own ends. He speaks well of "To the Sunset Breeze,"[31] where we find:

> Thou, laving, tempering all, cool-freshing, gently
> vitalizing
> Me, old, alone, sick, weak-down, melted-worn with
> sweat

where the collapse of syntax and idiom is only supportable because of varied strength of the beat. Even more of a similarity to *Propertius* can be sensed in the ending of "Song of Sunset":

> O setting sun! though the time has come,
> I still warble under you, if none else does, unmitigated
> admiration

where the stiltedness of "warble" and "unmitigated," the slightly ridiculous self-qualification of "if none else does," give the gamey flavour of typical Whitman. Allowing for the irony undercutting the afflatus, and heterosexual and not narcissistic overtones, isn't the residual voice of Whitman to be heard in such a line in *Propertius* as "I shall triumph among young ladies of indeterminate character"? And as for the bathetic mingling of grandiose proper nouns with the slang of the drug-store, isn't this to be found in "Song of the Exposition":

> Come Muse migrate from Greece and Ionia,
> Cross out please those immensely overpaid accounts,
> That matter of Troy and Achilles' wrath, and
> 　　Aeneas', Odysseus' wanderings

except that Pound's ear would not have suffered the awkward closing possessives? Tradition is not altogether a matter of personal choice, and this native American sound is one element of what Pound had for convertible energy.

For it is energy that subsumes Pound's approach to Provence, China, Rome. In those cultures, and their representative poets, he saw, as early as 1910, high development of technique and devotion to the common pre-occupations of mankind:

> What interest have all men in common? What forces
> play upon them all? Money and sex and tomorrow.[32]

Choosing to translate de Born, Rihaku and Propertius was in one respect to learn the most highly developed forms of melopoeia, phanopeia, and logopeia. Technique aside, these three poets, in particular, were chosen for their dedication to the attractions of the fair sex, and their wordly (*not* cynical) detachment towards positions of materialist love of money and status for its own sake. Like Heine and Gautier, like Golding and Gavin Douglas, other unlikely additions to Pound's great tradition, their dedication was above all a selfless one to the art of poetry. Technique was a life's work for Pound, and it was not a sterile pursuit: it is "the means of conveying an exact impression of exactly what one means in such a way as to exhilarate."[33] The sense of exhilaration is the real test. Impersonality is not it, literal exactitude neither. Propertius' "Ingenium nobis ipsa puella fecit" is certainly less jaunty than "My genius is no more than a girl" but the energy and the conviction, the universality of sexual and rhythmic impulse, still obtain. A sense of life, Pound was right in deciding, means its own sense of language.

Ian F. A. Bell

Mauberley's Barrier of Style

The ways in which we read *Hugh Selwyn Mauberley* are governed to a considerable extent by the framework of reference within which the poem operates; Pound's experience as an artist, literary journalist and entrepreneur, the battles over the visual arts and the state of a healthy literature, those figures who provide most of the poem's source material, in particular Flaubert, James, Gautier and De Gourmont, all contribute towards the efforts of critics to elucidate and to locate the poem. The reading experience demands a knowledge of an entire decade of notoriously difficult literary history. Now that much of the work of explication has been completed,[1] it is patently clear that the tensions and crises of that literary history have by no means resolved themselves into the kind of satisfying order that most critics seem to have found on behalf of the poem. Professor Espey's fundamental distinction, "the passive aesthete played off against the active instigator," still echoes ominously through later commentaries with only the isolated exception (that of Professor Rosenthal, for example). We are in the fortunate position of approaching *Mauberley* now with an immensely rich store of scholarly explication, but the decisions that have been made on the basis of that explication somehow obscure the reasons why the poem is "successful" or "good."

The "success" of *Mauberley* depends on the extent to

which we can read it as the portrait of the early struggles for
modernism during a period that was singularly unsym-
pathetic to such struggles. And more importantly, it must
be read as a portrait which is conceived in dramatic terms, as
a Vortex. For the poem to work in this way, the reader
cannot allow it to remain simply as a debate between "the
passive aesthete" and "the active instigator," because such a
perspective inevitably diminishes one half of the debate to
such an extent that the poem can only work as a biased
argument about aesthetics, with all the bias heavily in
favour of "the active instigator." The ease with which we
dismiss Mauberley as "the passive aesthete" is the ease with
which such a reading almost demands that we dismiss the
sequence as a whole. Pound understood the profound crisis
and ultimate exhaustion involved in the writer's resistance
to his age; crisis and exhaustion for which his own history
provides ample evidence. Mauberley's demise is the result
of such a crisis, his attempt and failure to follow certain
models; unless we see his temperament as considerably
more active than is usually allowed, the poem becomes
merely a shadowgraph of Pound's London experience, the
product of a tired mind no longer able to visualize the
battles of that experience.

The major task facing present readers of the poem is to
re-align the perspectives offered by the scholarship that
previous commentaries have provided. I want to concern
myself with suggesting ways in which Mauberley's creative
behavior, and the failure of that behavior, may be seen to be
the product of a situation of crisis. What is important about
Mauberley is not his failure in itself, but the reasons for that
failure, reasons which are primarily the result of choosing
the wrong tools whereby experience may be organized. He
is to be seen not as the passive dilutor of experience, but as a
figure whose attempts to deal with life result in a series of
barriers *against* life, methods of distance, rather than a
means for coming to terms *with* life; a secondary activity,
certainly, but it involves *effort* rather than mere susceptibil-

ity to delicate images. Mauberley is not so much seeking a style which will be adequate to a vision of experience as a style which will function at odds with the potential threat of that experience. The salient characteristic of the "Mauberley 1920" part of the sequence as a whole is the extraordinary system of polysyllabic vocabulary that is used to describe Mauberley's behavior. It is through a discussion of this system that I want to suggest how Mauberley attempts to place himself at a distance from potentially damaging experience, and that such an attempt involves considerably more activity than the behavior of a mere "impressionist"[2]; it is the result of a definite struggle, not of being simply overwhelmed by circumstance. I assume implicitly the arguments of earlier commentators for the proximity between Mauberley and Pound himself; the resonance and vitality of the poem rely exactly on this proximity. Mauberley "belongs" to Pound's own years of crisis, particularly the years of *Ripostes* (1911-1912), "The Wisdom of Poetry" (1912), "Psychology and Troubadours" (1912) and "The Serious Artist" (1913); it is no accident that the poem ends on an awkward ambiguity that is directly related to Pound's most acute efforts to confront "modernism" during this period.

I

The first major term of the vocabulary that is used on Mauberley's behalf is "phantasmagoria." The word is, as I have argued elsewhere ("The Phantasmagoria of Hugh Selwyn Mauberley", *Paideuma*, V. 3 [Winter, 1976], pp. 361-385), traditionally associated with an imaginative crisis of a particular kind; that of the interaction between a private, contemplative world of one's own ordering and a public actuality that is frequently hostile. There is an instance of the word's occurence which widens its field of reference in a way that is directly pertinent to the science-based nature of the rest of Mauberley's vocabulary. The word appears in one of Paul Elmer More's *Shelburne Essays,*

"The Quest of a Century" (1905);[3] taking his cue from
Dante, More is discussing the quest of the spirit for peace:

> We may find a people, such as the ancient Hindus, in
> whom the longing after peace was so intense as to make
> insignificant every other concern of life, and among
> whom the aim of saint and philosopher alike was to
> close the eyes upon the theatre of this world's shifting
> scenes. ...The spectacle of division and mutation be-
> came to them at last a mere phantasmagoria, like the
> morning mists that melt away beneath the upspringing
> day-star. (pp. 245–246)

"Phantasmagoria" suggests the insubstantiality of the actual
world; commonplace enough, but More goes on to discuss
the struggle between the will for permanence and the laws
of "division and mutation" within a context that is more
precise:

> ...nowhere is the conflict between the two principles
> more vividly displayed than in that battle between the
> followers of Xenophanes, who sought to adapt the
> world of change to their haunting desire for peace by
> denying motion altogether, and the disciples of
> Heraclitus, who saw only motion and mutation in all
> things and nowhere rest. "All things flow and nothing
> abides," said the Ephesian. ...(p. 246)

For Mauberley too, Heraclitean "flow" or, in modern terminology, "division and mutation," becomes a "phantasmagoria." But the interest of More's essay extends beyond
this kind of coincidence; he cites his material from pre-
Socratic philosophy as a prologue to the main theme of the
essay, the role of scientific investigation in the contemporary version of the conflict between order and mutability:

> ...we should call ours an age of observation. ...By long
> and intent observation of the phenomenal world the
> eye has discovered a seeming order in disorder. ...(pp.
> 200–201)

More recognizes the work of biologists as providing the

major instruments for making sense of natural process:

> Evolution is the living guide of our thought, assigning
> to the region of the unknowable the conceptions of
> unity and perfect rest, and building up its theories on
> the visible experience of motion and change and de-
> velopment. It has reduced the universal flux of Hera-
> clitus to a scientific system and assimilated it to our
> inner growth. ...(p. 253)

It should be obvious that Mauberley's polysyllabic vocabulary relies heavily on just such a method of science to deal
with the chaos of experience, yet commentators on the
poem have been curiously reluctant to expand on the
point.[4] It is exactly the indebtedness of Mauberley's vocabulary to ideas about scientific method that I want to devote
my attention; not only because the recognition of such an
indebtedness provides a clearer picture of Mauberley's aesthetics, but also because it defines the *kind* of barrier that
those aesthetics are able to construct against the phenomenal world conceived as a "phantasmagoria."

What saves More's essay from becoming simply another plea for the "Blessed rage for order" is precisely his
importing of ideas from contemporary science to reform
and rivivify a cultural program that is otherwise nothing
more than commonplace. Biological investigation deals
with the world of process by recognizing that change is the
fundamental characteristic of process and incorporating
change within its own laws. The most important effect of
this activity is to free the intellect from standard, and static,
procedures; More claims, for example, that with the aid of
the model from Evolution, we judge the past not "by an
immutable code" but "by reference to time and place" (p.
251), and so

> History was then no longer a mere chronicle of events
> or, if philosophical, the portrayal and judgement of
> characters from a fixed point of view; it became at its
> best the systematic examination of the causes of prog-
> ress and development. (pp. 251−252)

Significantly for Mauberley, More sees the application in
art of this intellectual freedom as resulting in impressionism, "the endeavor to reproduce what the individual
sees at the moment instead of a rationalized picture" (p.
252). Biology for More ensures that the past can no longer
be conceived as a discrete series of incidents, and that the
individual is released from fixed laws governing both his
life and his art. There are two points in More's thinking that
are relevant in general terms for a discussion of *Mauberley:*
first, the notion of scientific method as a counter to the
world of mutability; in his essay on "Victorian Literature"
(1910), More talks of the need

> to oppose to the welter of circumstance the force of
> discrimination and selection, to direct the aimless tide
> of change by reference to the co-existing law of the
> immutable fact, to carry the experience of the past into
> the diverse impulses of the present...[5]

Words like "discrimination" and "selection" offer key-
instruments for Mauberley's temperament. Secondly, in
the essay on "Criticism" of the same year, More makes his
most significant statement on the interaction between past
and present:

> The aim of culture is not to merge the present in a
> sterile dream of the past, but to hold the past as a living
> force in the present.[6]

What differentiates the past as "a sterile dream" from "a
living force" is More's understanding of biological evolution; the past remains "living" for the present through what
he calls "the larger race-memory."

More's position here is an elaboration of the
biological/aesthetic attitudes of Pater and Wilde, despite his
attempt in the essay to deny such an affiliation, and his
attitude towards the past clearly anticipates that of Pound
and Eliot who both rely on the vocabulary of biological
investigation to substantiate their traditionalism.[7] More's
gestures towards Pater and Wilde are particularly interest-

ing because I have always found it curious that neither of them are explicitly present in *Mauberley* (although the "lilies" in the opening "Ode" of the sequence certainly refers to Wilde via Pound's own early fascination with the literature of the eighties and nineties. The concern with art and beauty that he discovered in that literature announced a craftsmanship that for Pound was unavailable in an unprofessional America. Ford Madox Ford habitually used the image of the lily to differentiate the second-generation aestheticism of Wilde from "those robustious roarers," Rossetti, Morris and Hunt. Ford's distinction is one that for Pound would only come with experience; his youthful contact with literary London was a real attempt to wring "lilies from the acorn" in that it was a search for an idealism not encouraged by "a half savage country, out of date"). The absence of Pater and Wilde from the poem is odd not only because they anticipate some of Pound's own critical positions,[8] but also because they offer in so many ways the type for the situation of the minor artist. Most importantly, they provide the most obvious source and sanction for that vocabulary of Mauberley's which relies on the terminology of scientific investigation. I don't think it is claiming too much to assume that Pater and Wilde are the kind of figures that Mauberley would have read.

In his Preface to *The Renaissance,* Pater makes the analogy between the critic and the scientist: "His end is reached when he has disengaged that virtue, and noted it, as a chemist notes some natural element..." (pp. ix−x), a passage that Pound noted in the introduction to his translations of Cavalcanti.[9] Pater opens his final book, *Plato and Platonism* (1893) with a chapter on "Plato and the Doctrine of Motion," and, as Paul Elmer More is to do in "The Quest of a Century," he relates the operations of modern science back to the doctrine of Heraclitus:

> The entire modern theory of "development," in all its various phases, proved or unprovable,—what is it but old Heracliteanism awake once more in a new world,

and grown to full proportions. (Caravan Library edition, 1928, p. 13).

The tools with which we approach the world of flux must
then, of necessity, themselves partake of that world; Pater
says of Darwinsim: " 'type' itself properly is not but *is* only
always becoming" (p. 14). It is an interesting context for a
discussion of Platonic Idealism because, by analogy, biological laws are implicitly recognized as having an ontological
status similar to that of Plato's Ideas: they both offer a
measure of the immutable, and hence safety, against "the
wasting torrent of mere phenomena" (p. 21). Pater, the
master of a style developed to provide order for his personal chaos, invests that style with the authority of contemporary biology (the beauty of the "Mona Lisa" wrought out
"cell by cell") which is exactly Mauberley's "great affect."

Wilde, as is so often the case, exaggerates Pater's doctrine for his own purposes. What Wilde is seeking is ultimately an endorsement for contemplation,[10] and it is to this
end primarily that he relies on the sanction of science.
Anticipating Bergson and Hulme, Wilde claims in "The
Critic as Artist": "Action is limited and relative. Unlimited
and absolute is the vision of him who sits at ease and
watches, who walks in loneliness and dreams" (*Complete
Works*, ed. Holland, p. 1039). It is the contemplative mode
which leads to "the critical spirit," that hallmark of modernity which realizes "the collective life of the race," and what
makes the activity of the "critical spirit" possible is the
biological law of heredity: "By revealing to us the absolute
mechanism of all action...the scientific principle of heredity
has become, as it were, the warrant for the contemplative
life."

The principle of heredity serves to place the outer life,
the world of action, at a distance from the subjective vision,
a distance which reassuringly anaesthetises phenomenal
flux but which imports new dangers of its own; Wilde claims
of heredity that,

> ...while in the sphere of practical and external life it has robbed energy of its freedom and activity of its choice, in the subjective sphere, where the soul is at work, it comes to us, this terrible shadow, with many gifts in its hands, gifts of strange temperaments and subtle susceptibilities...complex multiform gifts of thoughts that are at variance with each other, and passions that war against themselves. (p. 1040)

I can think of no better description for Mauberley's "subjective hosannah"; his biological/aesthetic barrier of style against the external life precipitates a final crisis for the inner life: the operation of heredity provides the exotic grandeur of poem IV in the "Mauberley 1910" part of the sequence, but it is a grandeur which is too much at variance with itself, "A Consciousness disjunct," so that the result is an imaginative battle of the most intimate kind and finally suspension in the "vacant place" of the vortex. Mauberley is a figure who responds to the promise of Wilde's programme; the contemporaneity of all the ages:

> It [heredity] can help us to leave the age in which we were born, and to pass into other ages, and find ourselves not exiled from their air. It can teach us how to escape from our experience, and to realise the experience of those who are greater than we are. The pain of Leopardi crying out against life becomes our pain. Theocritus blows on his pipe, and we laugh with the lips of nymph and shepherd. In the wolfskin of Pierre Vidal we flee before the hounds... . Do you think that it is the imagination that enables us to live these countless lives? Yes; it is the imagination; and the imagination is the result of heredity. It is simply concentrated race-experience. (p. 1041).

But Mauberley forgets that the biological imagination is bought only at a price:

> ...it is not our own life that we live, but the lives of the dead, and the soul that dwells within us is no single

> spiritual entity, making us personal and individual,
> created for our service, and entering into us for our
> joy. It is something that has dwelt in fearful places, and
> in ancient sepulchres has made its abode. It is sick with
> many maladies, and has memories of curious sins. It is
> wiser than we are, and its wisdom is bitter. It fills us
> with impossible desires, and makes us follow what we
> know we cannot gain. (pp. 1040–1041)

The rhythm is Paterian, the muted exoticism anticipates the
"Portrait d'une Femme" from Pound's *Ripostes;* both hyp-
notize Mauberley into a fatal paralysis.[11]

For Wilde, the contemplative dream becomes translat-
able only through the "pose," a lesser version of Pound's
"persona": "to have a pose at all is something. It is a formal
recognition of the importance of treating life from a definite and reasoned standpoint" (p. 1042). Whereas the "persona" adopts a mask through which one speaks oneself, the
"pose" involves placing oneself at a distance from the object,
of being at a remove from it in order to offer an account
which is that of a spectator. The "pose" promises a release
from confrontation and effects between the observer and
the object what Wilde calls in "The Decay of Lying," "the
impenetrable barrier of beautiful style, of decorative or
ideal treatment" (p. 978). The passivity of the "pose" is not
that of being merely a "toy of circumstance"; it necessitates
an active moving away from experience, the creation of an
attitude from which to fictionalize about experience.
Mauberley's final crisis is not so much that he is subsumed
by his "subjective hosannah" as that the series of "poses" he
creates for himself are no longer adequate for the psychic
battles of an imagination evinced in hereditary terms.

The "fastidious rejection" that Wilde advocates on behalf of the "true critic" (p. 1041) has, in the context of "The
Critic as Artist" implications of a scientific "selection"; and
Wilde's "fastidious" directs us towards the Walter Villerant
of Pound's "Imaginary Letters" (1917–18), a figure who
similarly relies on the precepts of science:

If he would pick his company and then inebriate, instead of inebriating and then picking his company! In short if he weren't a dog-dasted fool, and likely to be a bore in all companies; if he weren't too full of sloth mental and physical to aspire to amateurs; if he would study the rudiments of physiognomy and make some sort of selection, SELECTION...[12]

Villerant is capable of using Pound's own science-based critical vocabulary: "The metal-finish alarms people. They will no more endure Joyce's hardness than they will Pound's sterilized surgery."[13] Villerant's usage is ambiguous, as Professor Davie has noted, and it is often impossible to determine with any precision the levels of irony and parody at which Pound is operating in the "Imaginary Letters." But Villerant does establish scientific axes for himself: "All things pass under the nose of my microscope."[14] What is interesting about this overtly "modernist" recognition is its air of being fashionable, and it is counterpointed by an exclusively decadent image of himself; Villerant's scientific distance from phenomena is apparent when he talks of "the reasonableness of reproducing the species," but he then goes on to plead:

My nerves, and the nerves of any woman I could live with three months, would produce only a victim— beautiful perhaps, but a victim; expiring of aromatic pain from the jasmine, lacking in impulse, a mere bundle of discriminations.[15]

The concern with nerves, the sense of recoil from sexual contact, "expiring of aromatic pain from the jasmine," all belong deceptively obviously to the popular image of the poets of the eighties and nineties.[16] Villerant's stance here is at such a remove from what happens in the other letters as to force quite crudely upon the reader a sense of his pose as the biological aesthete in the Wildean manner. "Selection," as I have already suggested, is a central term for the vocabulary of such a pose. It is a word that has ambiguous ramifications. One product of it is what Villerant calls "my

stratified culture,"[17] a phrase which occurs in the context of
a satire on the public taste for a standardized culture, a taste
exhibited in the proliferation of standard editions of various works and authors, with the corollary that what is lacking here is precisely any sense of selection.

For Villerant, "selection" ultimately becomes "fastidiousness"; it is this that he recommends to Lydia Burn when
she is thinking of remarrying: "there is a certain propreté, a
certain fastidiousness of the mind."[18] He gives an anecdote
concerning the mistress of a Viennese painter to illustrate
his understanding of the word:

> I can still hear her saying, as she waved a guardsman
> away from her table: "No, no, vot I say to dese people.
> Vot, I will zleep vit you. Yes, I vill zleep vit you. It is
> nossing. But talk to you half an hour. Neffair!! Vun
> musst traw de line SOMMEFVERE!!"

We need to be careful here; it is important to distinguish
between the fastidiousness of the intellect and sensibility
that Villerant advocates, and the fastidiousness of dress,
manner and speech that Pound found characteristic of the
Jamesian dilletante in 1912:

> One knows the type quite well. I have met "Osmond"
> in Venice. He ornamented leather. What most dis-
> tressed him in our national affairs was that Theodore
> Roosevelt had displayed the terrible vulgarity of ap-
> pearing at King Edward's funeral in a soft felt hat.[19]

The art of Mauberley, too, is that of ornamentation, but his
fastidiousness is that of Villerant rather than of the Jamesian aesthete as described by Pound. Villerant's fastidiousness certainly has its gesture towards the dilletante, but it
has its roots in the selection, the discrimination that Pound
is always demanding for the modern artist:

> Mr. Joyce's more rigorous selection of the presented
> detail marks him, I think, as belonging to my own
> generation, that is to the "nineteen-tens," not to the
> decade between "the nineties" and today.[20]

Pound's distinction between the "nineteen-tens," and the "decade between 'the nineties' and today," is one which neither Villerant nor Mauberley would be able to make; the case for "selection" is best put by A. R. Orage, echoing the Wilde of "The Critic as Artist" in claiming "Art, in short, is the discovery, maintenance, and culture of individuals," and that artists

> ...must never associate with the mob, they must be careful what they eat in the way of aesthetics; they must pick and choose among people, places and things with all the delicacy of an egg-shell among potsherds. Above all, they must keep their art pure.[21]

The biological Mauberley, in the tradition of a science used by Pater, Wilde and Villerant, is to be found primarily in poem II of the "Mauberley 1920" sequence. There, he is, in part, the botanist, seeking to "designate" his "new found orchid," seeking to erect a system of selection and nomenclature. The two key-words that define his situation are "precipitate" and "diastasis"; both belong to the terminology of biological chemistry, and both have a shared area of activity, that of a process of natural change. Mauberley "Drifted...drifted precipitate"; and the chemical meaning of "precipitate" is "To separate (a constituent) in solid form, as from a solution, usually by means of a reagent or heat." Not only does the word describe change, but its secondary meaning indicates a state of suspension: "To separate and fall, as a salt or substance which is held in solution." The word's implications are more fully expressed in "diastasis":

> He had passed, inconscient, full gaze,
> The wide-branded irides
> And botticellian sprays implied
> In their diastasis:

G. S. Fraser has noted the Empson-like difficulty of this stanza, and gives a good account of the way in which the chemical meaning of "diastasis" may be usefully incorporated into a reading of the poem.[22] He takes his definition

from Littré: "a soluble fermenting agent that transforms
various substances: ptyalin in the salivary gland is diastatic."
Strictly speaking, "diastasis" is a term from surgery: "The
separation of an epiphysis of a bone from its shaft; a dislo-
cation," but the Greek root in "diastase" allows its bio-
chemical meaning. To Fraser's definition, I would add that
of the *N.E.D.* for "diastase": "A nitrogenuous ferment
formed in a seed or bud during germination, and having
the property of converting starch into sugar."

The location of diastatic action specifically within the
period of germination postulates a more serious crisis on
Mauberley's part than simply the ignoring of a beautiful
woman or of a sexual invitation. The de Gourmont gloss for
the poem reminds us that the failure of biological recognition is concomitant with a failure of artistic recognition.
Through the poem's internal rhyme-scheme, "diastasis" is
connected with "anaesthesis" (itself reminiscent of the alco-
hol that "preserved" Lionel Johnson in "Sienna Mi Fe...");
for Mauberley, the "botticellian sprays" are trapped, anaesthetised, at the very moment of generation in nature, as the
stone dogs are trapped at the moment of transformation in
art, the high-point of the metamorphic process in which
Mauberley is suspended, rather as solid substance becomes
"held" in solution during precipitate action. The notion of
suspension elaborates the difficult opening line of poem II:
"For three years, diabolus in the scale." The reference to the
augmented fourth in music has been noted by Professor
Espey;[23] it is a reference which suggests not so much suspension as a precarious balance and it is, I think, in this
context, worth mentioning a possible play on the game of
"diabolo," defined by the *N.E.D.* as:

> An ancient game, newly revived, played by one or
> more persons, each of whom holds two sticks con-
> nected by a cord, on which is whirled a reel-like top.
> The point of this is to keep the reel spinning on the
> cord, to throw it up into the air and catch it again on the
> cord, or to pass it to and fro over a net...without allow-
> ing the reel to fall to the ground.

The mediary yet cacaphonic nature of the augmented fourth is visualized by the precarious balance of the reel that is only possible through the tenseness of the cord on which it spins. Together they offer a visual and auditory counterpart to the imaginative "phantasmagoria" that defines Mauberley's situation.

The bio-chemical states which elaborate this situation as confinement within the very moment of balance that instigates change, the precipitate and the diastatic, serve also to describe Mauberley's lexical efforts to deal with the world of process, of metamorphosis. Mauberley recognises that his scientific terminology must itself be not an abstract system of signs which by its nature is at odds with the world of flux, but an attempt syntactically to incorporate that flux within its own nomenclature. His limitation, and his crisis, is that he becomes trapped by the process immanent in such a nomenclature, confined by his own metalanguage.

Fundamentally, Mauberley chooses the wrong instrument for selecting, and hence controlling, phenomena. As the world of germination becomes increasingly threatening, he lacks a capacity for any effective use of the "sieve" and replaces it with the "seismograph." Mauberley's weighty progression from the one to the other is a move away from an instrument that is not only a mechanism for selection but that in another context functions as a mechanism for balance. At the end of his Postscript to Remy de Gourmont's *Natural Philosophy of Love*, Pound is concerned with the medium between asceticism and over-indulgence:

> The liquid solution must be kept at right consistency; one would say the due proportion of liquid to viscous particles, a good circulation; the actual quality of the sieve or separator, counting perhaps most of all; the balance and retentive media.[24]

The "balance" of separation here refers back to the affirmative effort to "precipitate"; as Mauberley's "sieve" becomes his "seismograph," that affirmation is replaced by the confinement of an anaesthetised "diastasis." The Postscript to *The Natural Philosophy of Love* indicates Pound's own awareness of the potential danger of the effort to achieve "balance"; the man who can control his sperm is "the talented sieve," but "the suspended spermatozoid...is ready to dispense with, in the literal sense, incarnation, enfleshment."[25] In a wider context, Henri Poincaré uses the term "delicate sieve" to describe the principle of selection governing mathematical thought. His argument is for the "special aesthetic sensibility" of mathematics as opposed to the notion of mathematics as a discipline which merely applies mechanical rules. It is exactly this "sieve" that defines for Poincaré the real work of discovery.[26]

Mauberley's progression, then, is from a naturalistically viable method of discrimination to one that bears all the weight of the exact sciences, an instrument that can account for the relative qualities of phenomena but only within a very narrow range, "Of eye-lid and cheek-bone." As biology results in confinement, Mauberley puts his faith in the abstractions of exact science in order to survive. As "sieve" becomes "seismograph," as we move from poem II to the increased pressures of poem III, "The Age Demanded," so Mauberley's vocabulary becomes increasingly abstract, a vocabulary of measurement only.

II

The world revealed by the physics of the late nineteenth and early twentieth centuries was chaotic beyond anyone's expectations, but the physicist's response to flux was rather different from that of the biologist to natural process. Whereas the biologist attempted to incorporate relational process into his nomenclature, no such attempt was possible for the physicist. He recognised that nature could no longer be seen as constituted by the enduring objects of traditional physics,[27] and so conceived his task to be "description" rather than "explanation" of the phenomenal world. Henry Adams, faced with the world of twentieth century physics, understood that the historian's concern was not so much with factual truth or factual knowledge, but with measurement:

> The historian never stopped repeating to himself that he knew nothing about it; that he was a mere instrument of measure, a barometer, pedometer, radiometer; and that his whole share in the matter was restricted to the measurement of thought-motion as marked by the accepted thinkers. He took their facts for granted.[28]

Clearly, the science that announces "description" rather than "explanation" is laudable enough; it is an honest recognition not only of the nature of the physical world but of the extent and possibilities of its methods for dealing with that world. Like all the other models offered for Mauberley, it has affirmative strength but also potential danger.

The main impetus for the notion of science as descriptive rather than explanatory came from the Reductionist school of physicists who were deeply influential during the period between 1880 and 1930. Their main voice was that of the German physicist, Ernst Mach, but their theories became most widely spread, in England at least, through a book by one of Mach's disciples, Karl Pearson, *The Grammar of Science* (1892). A considerable part of Mauberley's problem is that most of the major popular discussions of scientific method around and following the turn of the century were all concerned to deny its mechanistic world-view and hence its comfort and safety; Thorstein Veblen described the intellectual shifts thus:

> The dramatic interpretation of natural phenomena has thereby become less anthropomorphic; it no longer contrasts the life-history of a cause working to produce a given effect—after the manner of a skilled workman producing a piece of wrought goods—but it constructs the life-history of a process in which the distinction between cause and effect need scarcely be observed in an itemised and specific way, but in which

the run of causation unfolds itself in an unbroken
sequence of cumulative change.[29]

Mauberley's manner is very much that of the "skilled
workman producing a piece of wrought goods," but clearly
such a manner is, to say the least, dangerously out of date.
So, a different rationale for scientific method has to be
invented, and clearly the postulation of science as simply a
different language for describing the world, instigated by
the Reductionist thinkers, solved most of science's epis-
tomological problems at one blow. Once the scientist is
conceived solely as a descriptive measuring instrument,
then he is immediately freed from the burden of explanation and he is enabled to remove himself from the active
world; as Pearson notes: "The scientific man has above all
things to strive at self-elimination in his judgements."[30] For
Pound, of course, such anonymity provides the basis for the
ethics of science and for the seriousness of literature but for
Mauberley it offers the prime sanction for self-evasion, for
the construction of elaborate barriers for self-protection.

Scientific method as a linguistic structure is directly
relevant for Pound himself; Pearson maintains that a scientific "law" is only meaningful in the sense that it is "a résumé
in mental shorthand, which replaces for us a lengthy description of the sequences among our sense impressions,"[31]
which is exactly the basis for Fenollosa's version of the
ideogram: "a vivid shorthand picture of the operations in
nature" (Fenollosa, of course, was, for Pound, the first man
to apply scientific method to literary criticism). There is no
question of moving from description to explanation because science "asserts no perceptual reality for its own
shorthand."[32] So, science is to be considered not as a guide
to any further reality, but as an economical lexical instrument for organizing our sensations with respect to external
phenomena. Apart from Pearson, the most influential
explicator of such a position for the popular mind was the
French mathematician, Henri Poincaré; almost the whole
of La Valeur de la Science (Paris, 1905) is devoted to the view

that the various theories offered by science are to be understood as different languages for describing the facts.

Poincaré, of all the theorists, is concerned to see scientific method as imaginative. The "beauty" of scientific research is revealed in the harmony of nature that it discovers:

> It is this that gives a body a skeleton, so to speak, to the shimmering visions that flatter our senses, and without this support the beauty of these fleeting dreams would be imperfect, because it would be indefinite and ever elusive.[33]

The same "beauty" governs the principles of selection, since those facts are chosen which are best suited to contribute to such harmony, and it governs the economy of scientific description:

> ...care for the beautiful leads us to the same selection as care for the useful. Similarly economy of thought, that economy of effort which, according to Mach, is the constant tendency of science, is a source of beauty as well as a practical advantage.[34]

Poincaré's mathematical aestheticism with its harmonious order would have been more than sufficient to seduce Mauberley, paralysed by his biological enterprise and desperately in need of a new model. Just as biology contains its dangers within its own methodology, so too do the procedures of the exact sciences as evinced by Pearson and Poincaré. For Pound, both the value and the danger of the material I have been describing may be seen most clearly in two areas; the attitude of T. E. Hulme towards science, and a strange monograph by Hudson Maxim, *The Science of Poetry and the Philosophy of Language* (1910).

Maxim's book contains much that is of interest to Pound; in his Introduction, Maxim sets up one of his major premises:

> The great naturalist requires but a few pieces of bone from any prehistoric monster in order to ascertain

> whether it was herbivorous or carnivorous, reptile or
> mammal, or even to construct a counterpart of its
> entire skeleton.[35]

It is a familiar enough story, perennially fascinating for the
layman; Wilde uses it at the end of "The Critic as Artist,"
and it provides the basis of Pound's admiration for figures
like Agassiz and Frobenius. One of Maxim's main arguments is referred to Spencer's "The Philosophy of Style"
(1852), rather than to Pearson, for reasons, I suspect, of
academic pedantry; this is the argument that "language...is
most nearly perfect when it is of the simplest construction
and does its work with the least expenditure of energy."[36]
Maxim goes on to see language not only as economizing
mental activity, but also energizing it,[37] notions which are,
of course, central for the Vorticist poet. As far as Mauberley
is concerned, economy is attractive, but energy is beyond his
capacity.

    Pound refers to Maxim's book in two places:[38] he re-
views it in 1910, and two years later, although he omits to
signify it as other than "A book which was causing some
clatter about a year ago," Pound begins his important "The
Wisdom of Poetry" by citing what he considers to be
Maxim's most important definition:

> Poetry is the expression of imaginative thought by
> means only of the essentials to the thought, conserving
> energy for thought-perception, to which end all ani-
> mate, inanimate and tangible things may assume the
> properties and attributes of tangible, living, thinking
> and speaking things, possessing the power of becom-
> ing what they seem, or of transfiguration into what
> they suggest.[39]

Here, precisely, is the potency of metamorphosis that
energizes Pound and finally paralyses Mauberley. Maxim's
definition provides the main value of the book for Pound
who in both essays derides Maxim's style, bad taste and
pomposity; there is a guarded approbation for the energy
and the effort to be "scientific," a guardedness which

emerges in: "I would rather have my poetry read by someone who had read Maxim than by someone who had read
no criticism of poetry."[40]

Maxim's treatise is, as Pound says, a curiosity, indeed
frequently simply ridiculous; but it does play a larger role in
Pound's critical thinking than he seems prepared to admit.
Pound declares that it contains "much that is worth reading," and certainly in "The Wisdom of Poetry," Maxim's
model for literary criticism serves to instigate one of
Pound's most revealing analogies, that between the poet
and the abstract mathematician:

> What the analytical geometer does for space and form,
> the poet does for the states of consciousness. ...By the
> signs $a^2 + b^2 = c^2$, I imply the circle. By $(a-r)^2 +
> (b-r)^2$, I imply the circle and its mode of birth. I am led
> from the consideration of the particular circles formed
> by my ink-well and my table-rim, to the contemplation
> of the circle absolute, its law; the circle free in all space,
> unbounded, loosed from the accidents of time and
> space.[41]

Both the poet and the scientist are conceived as reaching a
point where they can dispense with the factual limitations of
the phenomenal world and approach an Absolute; the "accidents of time and space" match the "discouraging doctrine of chances" that is so disconcerting for Mauberley: the
formulae of geometry offer the possibility of protection
against the unique, the unexpected. The mixed vocabulary
of the essay, from geometry, religious mysticism, Platonic
Idealism, illustrates Pound's own efforts towards solidify-
ing his critical terminology, anticipating the confused mixture of the more famous "Psychology and Troubadours," a
few months later (October, 1912). Pound's struggle is not
fully resolved until the "Vorticism" essay of 1914, but there
is a very interesting piece of 1913 which gives a marvellously
comic parody of exactly the "scientific" method for literary
criticism.[42] He constructs a "table of opinions" to cover the
range of judgments prevalent in contemporary literary

journalism; the "scientific norm" that Pound proposes
works according to the principle that "there are only a
certain number of things that can be said about a book," and
given the list of these opinions, the reviewer may save a lot
of time and energy by slipping any new book into the
prepared slot. Clause six, for example, erects standards of
comparison: "Mr. Figgis considers that the merits of this
author, while approaching those of Frank Harris, Abercrombie and Shakespeare, do not in all points attain those
of Mr. Abercrombie." The absurd logic reaches its climax as
Pound concludes by inverting that logic:

> It will be seen that we have here the opinions if not of
> all the leaders of thought at least of leaders who are
> typical of all the brands of thought now thought in
> England. As the number of clauses which apply to any
> given possible book is very greatly in excess of the
> number of those which do not apply, the reviews will
> consist simply of the numerals belonging to the clauses
> which do NOT apply.[43]

Wittily and economically Pound satirizes not only contemporary conventions of criticism but also his own ambitions
for a "scientific norm," for a series of "measuring rods," of
axes of reference that would have the capacity to weigh
Theocritus and Yeats in one balance. That he can lampoon
such ambitions so effectively demonstrates not only his own
increasing control over "scientific" method, but also his
awareness of its potential limitations. By the time of the
"Vorticism" essay a year later, the argument in "The Wisdom of Poetry" is substantiated more completely and more
consistently by the vocabulary from mathematics; the earlier struggle, the confusion is gone. It is here that we find
the most forceful possibility for control over, and distance
from, the "accidents," the "discouraging doctrine of
chances" in the phenomenal world:

> The statements of "analytics" are "lords" over fact.
> They are the thrones and dominations that rule over
> form and recurrence. And in like manner are great

works of art lords over fact, over race-long recurrent
moods, and over tomorrow.[44]

The infamous "counter-language" of T. E. Hulme involves the clearest account of that view of scientific method
which understands science as providing descriptions of the
world in terms of stasis, at a distance from process. For
Hulme, this kind of description exhibits the limitations of
science, but for Mauberley it promises the necessary barriers of protection against the chance-oriented world of
process:

> By constant elimination
> The manifest universe
> Yielded an armour
> Against utter consternation,

The principle of "selection" by now is refined to "elimination." Hulme, unlike Bergson, takes little account of biology
and constructs his arguments for a "counter-language" on
the distances implicit in the exact sciences, their removal
from the "durée réele," precisely as Mauberley is to use the
exact sciences to deal with his confinenement in metamorphosis. Just as Mauberley is trapped by the metamorphosis
of biology, so he becomes trapped by the metasymbolism of
the exact sciences.

Hulme had read *The Grammar of Science* at school and
disliked it.[45] His understanding of science is almost wholly
informed by the arguments of Pearson's book; Hulme sees
science as providing an alternative terminology for
phenomena, a terminology consisting in static and inflexi-
ble symbols whose only function is for purposes of convenience, of "getting about," and hence is totally abstract. He is
unwilling to translate the measuring function of scientific
symbols into anything more fruitful; scientific measurement for Hulme is never other than a substitutive symbolism. These symbols, "counters," are only definable and
meaningful in terms of other "counters"; they remain trapped in the system to which they belong, with no reference to
the process of actual life. In stressing the importance of

"Seeing 'solid' things," Hulme offers as a counterpoint an "Analysis of the attitude of a man reading an argument":

> Compare in algebra, the real things are replaced by symbols. These symbols are manipulated according to certain laws which are independent of their meaning. N. B. At a certain point in this proof we cease to think of 'x' as having a meaning and look upon it as a mere counter to be manipulated.[46]

His attitude is best summarized in the following passage from "Cinders":

> The aim of science is to reduce the complex and inevitably disconnected world of grit and cinders to a few ideal counters, which we can move about and so form an ungritlike picture of reality—one flattering to our sense of power over the world.[47]

III

It is Hulme's notion of rigid formalization that finally appeals to Mauberley; the possibility of locating himself as a scientific observer at a distance from phenomena and thereby achieving that quality of certainty which his experience lacks. Mauberley's view of science, from the position of being "Caught in metamorphosis," suspended in biological process, is to see it as a way of nullifying that process by treating objects in isolation, at moments of stasis. His impoverished understanding of the comparative method in poem II, "the relation/Of eyelid and cheek-bone," is replaced by his "sense of graduations," his "constant elimination" and "selected perceptions" in poem III, as he moves from the flux of biology to the supposed certainty of the exact sciences in his efforts towards schematization, Villerant's "stratified culture."

The possibilities for scientific behavior that the poem sets up have nothing to do with the mechanism/vitalism debate that bedeviled much of nineteenth-century science.

By the time of *Mauberley*, the Reductionist thinkers had made that issue simply out of date. Karl Pearson's Introduction to *The Grammar of Science* makes the point abundantly clear:

> Step by step men of science are coming to recognize that mechanism is not at the bottom of phenomena, but is only the conceptual shorthand by aid of which they can briefly describe and resume phenomena... . All science is description and not explanation.[48]

Scientific method ensures the spectatorial distance that Mauberley needs; descriptive measurement provides the starting point and the scientist then moves on to offer a conclusion about these measurements: Mauberley never moves beyond the stage of measurement. It is appealing because it seems to remove the obligation to action, to actually say anything. Mauberley's vocabulary is that of a metalanguage and he remains confined by his descriptive symbolism; Sir Arthur Eddington, one of the great popularizers of scientific method, points out in his mainly retrospective Gifford Lectures of 1927: "Science aims at constructing a world which shall be symbolic of the world of commonplace experience."[49] Mauberley's world is "symbolic" in the sense suggested by Eddington; the style of his scientific vocabulary creates a "meta-world" whose terms have no reference outside its own frame of meaning. The rhyme-scheme that oppressively dominates this vocabulary defines the closed nature of Mauberley's style which, in the absense of any external point of contact, has no choice but to turn in on itself. Mauberley's failure is a failure to move beyond the measurements registered by his "seismograph" and to break the rhyme-scheme that confines the style through which he seeks protection. Eddington summarises the initial limitations of the scientific measuring process:

> Whether we are studying a material object, a magnetic field, a geometrical figure, or a duration of time, our scientific information is summed up in measures... .

> We feel it necessary to concede some background to
> the measures—an external world—but the attributes
> of this world, except in so far as they are reflected in
> the measures, are outside scientific scrutiny. Science
> has at last revolted against attaching the exact knowl-
> edge contained in these measurements to a traditional
> picture-gallery of conceptions which convey no au-
> thentic information of the background and obtrude
> irrelevancies into the scheme of knowledge.[50]

This scrupulous distance is the triumph of science's
account of the phenomenal world, but for Mauberley, the
metalanguage through which he attempts to create such a
distance on his own behalf results in his confinement in that
linguistic style itself. To adopt a word used by Eddington,
Mauberley constructs a "shadowgraph" of actual experience, a shadowgraph that corresponds exactly with Pound's
description of Euclidean geometry:

> ...one has begun to talk about form... . But even this
> statement does not *create* form... . Statements in plane
> or descriptive geometry are like talk about art. They
> are a criticism of the form. The form is not created by
> them.[51]

Mauberley's vocabulary should be seen in the context I
have been describing. His efforts to come to terms with the
world after the biological manner of Pater or Wilde in poem
II results in his confinement within metamorphic process.
His reliance on the exact sciences in poem III (his "sense of
graduations," the instruments of "elimination" "isolation"
and "selected perceptions," set against the "discouraging
doctrine of chances" and the "unexpected palms," the
chance or accident orientated world of the unique for which
science can never ascribe a place), results in "A consciousness disjunct," Mauberley poised between the "either" and
the "or"; a paralysis not within the germinal centre of
change, but within the static objects created by his own style,
"...this overblotted / Series / Of intermittences." The

models from scientific method that Mauberley chooses exhibit ambiguities similar to those of the figures of James, Flaubert and Gautier in the poem. It is the achievement of *Mauberley* to explore the tensions which constitute the fabric of these ambiguities, tensions which discourage any reading of the poem as simply a dichotomized drama of aesthetic theory. The struggle is manifest through such tensions; the poem is a drama of emotions that is concerned with the possibilities available to a certain mode of imaginative behavior during a period of crisis.

Walter Baumann

The Structure of Canto IV

Remembering the anecdote of Agassiz and the fish, as told by Ezra Pound in the *ABC of Reading*, I felt the urge to do to Canto IV what Agassiz had wanted his graduate student to do to the sunfish all along: to begin, not by classifying and by making a number of abstract statements about it, but by actually looking at it.

There are 758 words in Canto IV. This is roughly the standard length of most early Cantos. When Pound was recording Canto IV for Caedmon it took him seven minutes and eighteen seconds to produce, in Harvey Gross's words, a "beautifully stylized chant which holds firmly to metrical bedrock."[1] So it is not surprising that the speed was about one sixth under the normal broadcasting rate for talks, but it was a good quarter faster than when Basil Bunting was reading half of Canto IV for the BBC. According to the composer himself, then, the correct chanting speed is about 140 syllables per minute, certainly not Largo, as with Bunting, but perhaps Adagio.

Of the 1049 syllables 472 receive stress in Pound's declamation. This might suggest that we are not far from the traditional alternating verse, but a look at the division into lines will tell otherwise. Since there are 128 lines the average number of syllables per line is just over eight. The actual range is from two syllables ("Ityn" *ll.* 16 & 20) to seventeen, in "Vidal, or Ecbatan, upon the gilded tower in Ecbatan" (*l.* 117). The majority of lines, however, have

between five to nine syllables (83), with the seven-syllable
line as the most frequent type (24), followed by the line with
eight syllables (17), the one with six (15), the one with nine
(14) and the one with five (13). The eleven-syllable line
occurs twelve times but since the ten-syllable line is used
only six times, it does not belong to the majority group any
more. So only one sixth of all lines could be pentameters of
the alternating type at all. To see whether there are any
indeed we must consider the distribution of the stresses.
The average is three and a half (3.65) stresses per line. In
actual fact, the lines with three stresses make up almost one
third of the Canto (41), the lines with four stresses about a
quarter (30). The five-stress line comes next with twenty
occurrences, then the two-stress line with eighteen. Look as
we may, there is not one regular iambic pentameter among
the lines with five stresses. Of the seven lines which have
either ten or eleven syllables only three come at all close to
one. They all have masculine endings, so that the extra
syllable introduces an anapaest into the iambic pattern:

> | The va | lley is thick | with leaves, | with leaves, | the
>   trees | (*l.* 35),
> | The emp | ty ar | mour shakes | as the cyg | net moves |
>   (*l.* 68),
> | As Gy | ges on Thra | cian pla | tter set | the feast |
>   (*l.* 114).

The appearance of only one trisyllabic foot in a line is an
acceptable license even in a poem wholly in blank verse, but
it is certainly true to say that in the rest of Canto IV the
dominance of the verse line which was synonymous with
English poetry for so long is effectively broken, and very
consciously so, for the line from Canto LXXXI seems to
refer to the writing of a text like ours:

> (To break the pentameter, that was the first heave)
>   (518:553)

The celebrated imagistic line, "The scarlet flower is cast on the blanch-white stone" (*l.* 88) is one step further away from the alternating pattern, in that there are two anapaests. But the line furthest away from traditional English verse is the one with six stresses, yet only eight syllables:

|Beat, beat,| whirr, thud,| in the soft turf (*l.* 8)

Apart from "in the" all syllables not only carry stress, but can also be called long. Stress and quantity, in the rare cases where the existence of the quantitative principle can in fact be proved beyond all reasonable doubt, do not conflict with each other, but, as appears to be the rule with Pound, join to create verse of a most astonishing limpidity.[2] Our line is of course only possible because it moves outside normal human speech into interjection-like onomatopoeia. But the spondee is certainly much in evidence throughout Canto IV, in particular at the end of verse lines: "soft turf" (*l.* 8), "sea-foam" (*l.* 12), "the slim white| stone bar" (*l.* 25), "firm| pale stone" (*l.* 27) "and the| air, air" (*l.* 44), "wheat swath" (*l.* 61), "spring's mouth" (*l.* 76), "king's wind" (*l.* 90), "earth's bag" (*l.* 94) and "earth loam" (*l.* 126). Hugh Kenner has gone as far as to consider such endings the most conspicuous part of Pound's metrical signature.[3]

It is the spondees, then, which make the proportion between the total number of syllables and the number of stresses look like that encountered in alternating verse. They hide, as it were, Pound's trisyllabic feet. In Canto IV there are just about 150 trisyllabic elements, and about fifteen of these we should perhaps call tetrasyllabic. At any rate roughly half of Canto IV is either dactylic or anapaestic, and the majority of lines have at least one trisyllabic element. However, those with more than two are rare, the main ones being "Anaxi| forminges!| Auruncu|leia" (*l.* 3) and "Not a ray,| not a sli|vver,|| not a spare| disc of sun|light" and its two variants (*ll.* 41, 51 & 55). The iambs and trochees, which simply cannot be avoided in a language like English and are therefore fairly frequent even in Pound, are often drowned by the might of the spondees, so that what we are left with is indeed, as Harvey Gross confirms and as Kenner would agree, although he mainly speaks of the spondees, Pound's unmistakable prosodical signature, "the dactylic-anapaestic and spondaic paradigms."[4] As the best examples in Canto IV Gross singles out the onomatopoeic "Beat, beat,| whirr, thud,| in the soft turf" (*l.* 8) and the second line of what I have called the Dawn Lyric,[5] the full text of which is:

> The sil| ver mi| rrors catch| the bright| stones and|
>   flare,
> Dawn, to our| waking,| drifts in the| green cool | light;
> Dew-haze| blurs, in the| grass, pale | ankles| moving.
> Beat, beat,| whirr, thud,| in the soft turf
>   under the a| pple trees,
> Choros nym| pharum,| goat-foot,| with the pale| foot
>   alter| nate;
> Crescent of| blue-shot| waters,| green-gold| in the
>   sha| llows,
> A black| cock crows| in the sea-| foam. (*ll.* 5–12)

The beginning is almost an iambic pentameter. But "bright stones" is, from the point of view of strictly alternating verse, literally the "stone of stumbling, the rock of offense." Although the second line still has five feet, we now make out a dactyl, a trochee (alas!), a dactyl, a spondee and the first half of another. The escape from, as Gross puts it, "the iambic domination which had crippled the long poem since Milton"[6] is crowned by full success.

From syllables to words. There are no doubt whole lessons to be learnt from a study of the phonology and morphology of Pound's words. The only reason for its omission here is lack of time and patience, and in the hope that the gap will be filled some day, I proceed directly to an assessment of the vocabulary in Canto IV. Most of the words are perfectly ordinary, neither specially poetic, except perhaps in the combinations "Golden Prows" (*l.* 4), "cast her down" (*l.* 11), "all the while" (*l.* 19), "a-top" (*l.* 36), "white-gathered" (*l.* 44), "Shadow'd, o'ershadow'd" (*l.* 49) and "blanch-white" (*l.* 88), nor antiquated, except possibly the "but" in "Troy but a heap" (*l.* 2) and in "Hither, hither" (*l.* 58) as a shout used by men out hunting. This may suggest that by the time he wrote Canto IV Pound did understand something of the "meaning of 'Wardour Street.' "[7] Nor is there much specialized vocabulary. The only items that catch the eye are "splotch" (*l.* 51) and "shatter" (*l.* 51) for fragments of light, and "sheaf" (*l.* 60) and "swath" (*l.* 61) for the heap of hair that turns into gold. The specialization is taken care of by the foreign language expressions, a mere seven of them, by the thirteen geographical names and by the seventeen names of persons or deities, a most untypical state of affairs, if we think of all the rest of the *Cantos*. Considering that of the 37 names and foreign phrases the average reader might know as many as half, it is strange that even such a "simple" Canto continues to baffle layman and expert alike. And, indeed, this bewilderment is far more due to the syntax than to the vocabulary.

Of the 128 lines as many as 50 have no verb at all. There are whole stretches of three, once even four lines, without a single verb. There is no verb in the three opening lines, none for four lines after "Hither, hither, Actaeon" (*ll.* 58−61) and none in both groups of lines culminating in "beneath the knees of the gods" (*ll.* 70−72 & 79−81). Only in four of the six run-on lines do we find a verb as link:

> the slim white stone bar
> Making a double arch (*ll.* 25−26)
> and the wind out of Rhodez
> Caught in the full of her sleeve. (*ll.* 29−30)
> The pines at Takasago
> grow with the pines of Isé! (*ll.* 74−75)

> Not a ray, not a slivver, not a spare disc of sunlight
> Flaking the black, soft water (*ll.* 41–42)

On the other hand, there are eight lines with two verbs and two lines with three:

> Lifting, lifting and waffing (*l.* 47)
> Thus the light rains, thus pours, *e lo soleils plovil* (*l.* 69)

Of the 78 lines with verbs 24, or one third, are nevertheless elliptical or fragmentary from a syntactical point of view, because they have no finite verb, but only either a present participle (24) or a past participle (4). Since only 54 lines contain full sentences we can safely say that the grammatical fragment predominates by nearly two to one. William E. Baker, statistically analysing Canto IV as well as Canto II, found the ratio to be even more than two to one, and he comments:

> Obviously, Pound has attempted what none of his five famous predecessors [Bryant, Longfellow, Arnold, Tennyson and Swinburne] dared, the construction of poems (or large, unified sections of poems) primarily out of fragments.[8]

The loss of explicitness resulting from syntactical fragmentation is clearly at the bottom of many a comprehension difficulty, but it can also stimulate increased audience involvement. Moreover, it can be of benefit to an author like Pound who wishes to blur the difference between the past and the present. Since the events described and alluded to in Canto IV belong to a consciousness which believes all ages to be "contemporaneous"[9] they may as well be told in the present tense as in the past tense. There was no real need for Pound to use the past tense in telling Soremonda's suicidal jump from the window (*ll.* 18–32). Clearly the present tense would not do with the mention of Cavalcanti ("As Cavalcanti had seen her" *l.* 125), or would it? In connection with Père Henri Jacques, Pound originally had "Père Henri Jacques still seeks the sennin,"[10] subsequently changing it to "Père Henri Jacques would speak with the sennin" (*l.* 111), but when he was quoting himself in Canto LXXXVIII he used the present tense again:

> Père Henri Jacques still
>   speaks with the sennin on Rokku (582:618).

As the Wind Interlude (*ll.* 89−99) is for the most part in dialogue form a decision as to the tense is only required in the two lines introducing the speakers. To this day the Faber edition has "That Ran-ti opened his collar" (*l.* 93), whereas *Poems 1918–1921* had "And Ran-ti, opening his collar," the version still printed in the New Directions text and the one Pound used when recording for Caedmon. The use of the present participle, in other words, introduces a welcome ambiguity as to the time level of the event told.

One of the few transitional devices Pound uses in Canto IV is "and," not as a true conjunction, but normally as a kind of metrical upbeat, akin to the biblical "And it came to pass." According to Goodwin, such "ands" can now be found in other authors and may be traced back to Pound.[11] It is the type of "and" which we find not only at the beginning of Canto I, but at the beginning of almost one sixth of all Cantos.[12] Five of the eight "ands" which are used in this upbeat fashion in our Canto mark the beginning of every fifth line from "And by the curved, carved foot" to "and a valley" (*ll.* 13−34). Although it is going too far to say that these twenty lines are thus split up into four five-line stanzas, since there is no further repeat of any kind in them apart from the doubling of "And she went toward the window" (*ll.* 18 & 24), this is the only quantifiable prosodical regularity in the whole of this Canto, and a very easily missed one at that. In the New Directions text we find two more Poundian "ands" at an interval of five lines:

> And Sō-Gyoku, saying (*l.* 89)
> And Hsiang, opening his collar (*l.* 93)

but this would be of no significance whatever if we had not noticed the previous five-line pattern. We note in passing that *Poems 1918–1921* has, instead of one of those "ands," "meanwhile" at the beginning of the Wind Interlude. The final "and" of this type introduces the presence of spectators, turning the Canto into a tragedy watched in an amphitheatre like that in Verona:

> And we sit here...
>   there in the arena... (*ll.* 127–28).

This announcement could easily have been used at the very beginning of the Canto, as indeed it is at the beginning of Canto XII, where it provides a most incongruous setting for the telling of the story of Baldy Bacon and the story of the Honest Sailor.

Typographically Canto IV is divided into seven sections of varying length, the shortest section being seven lines, the longest 44. There is obviously no pattern emerging. Unless there is an "and" at the start, as in the second and (at least in the New Directions text) the fifth section, there is nothing specifically telling us that we are now facing a new scene. Hence we must be grateful for the lines which Pound must have instructed the printer to leave blank. The fourth section starts with a "thus," which could be called a variation of the Poundian "and." The section endings, however, are clearly marked. There is fade-out in the two final sections, indicated by dots ("Gray stone-posts leading..." [*l.* 110]; "And we sit here.../there in the arena..." [*ll.* 127–28]. There are rounding-off phrases at the end of the second and the fourth sections ("the pale hair of the goddess" [*l.* 56]; "beneath the knees of the gods" [*l.* 81], but in the three remaining cases a change occurs from the open and fragmentary syntax to what the grammarian calls the regular one:

> A black cock crows in the sea-foam (*l.* 12)
> The empty armour shakes as the cygnet moves (*l.* 68)

> The scarlet flower is cast on the blanch-white
>   stone (*l.* 88)

Earl Miner has called such lines "superpository images" or
"unifying metaphors" and they are of course a reminder of
the imagist Ezra Pound, where the "superpository image,"
as the most famous example demonstrates, does not necessarily have to be a full sentence:

> The apparition of these faces in the crowd;
> Petals on a wet, black bough.

It is curious to think that the sentence "The empty armour
shakes as the cygnet moves" is the most elaborate syntactical
structure in the whole of Canto IV. The only other subor-
dinate clauses, apart from one clause of concession ("If it
were gold" [*l.* 39]), are also introduced by "as" and are
likewise adverbial clauses, not of time but of manner:

> Blue agate casing the sky (as at Gourdon that
>   time) (*l.* 84),
> As Gyges on Thracian platter set the feast (*l.* 114),
> As Cavalcanti had seen her (*l.* 25).[13]

Apart from one solitary "or" ("Vidal, or Ecbatan" [*l.* 117]),
there is only one more connective particle used in our text.
This is one that, according to most theorists, should not
occur any more in modern poetry: the preposition "like."
Pound, as "In a Station of the Metro" shows, seems to fit this
rule. All the same "like" occurs in Canto IV five times. In the
case where he makes a comparison between the roof
formed by the leaves and two other types of roofs ("a fish-
scale roof" and "the church roof in Poictiers" [*ll.* 36 & 37])
the avoidance of "like" would very likely make it impossible
for the reader to see that a comparison was intended. If one
of the intentions of the poet is to use the natural language,
he cannot very well further qualify the adjective "thick"
without adding "like," as Pound does in "Thick like a wheat
swath" (*l.* 61) and "thick like paint" (*l.* 120). In connection

with "Moves like a worm, in the crowd" (*l.* 122) Pound, as if indeed battling against the word "like", originally wrote:

> The worm of the Procession bores in the soup of the
>   crowd

but he obviously decided later that it was too "rich" and humbly accepted the services of "like." Moreover, "Moves like a worm" may be intended as an echo to that very prominent line in Canto II:

> Moves, yes she moves like a goddess (6:10).

For the rest the syntax in Canto IV is plainly paratactical, even in the dialogue of the Wind Interlude where the conjunction "because" could have been used quite naturally (e.g., "This wind belongs to the palace/Because it shakes imperial water-jets"). In the middle range of the Canto the parataxis is modified, however, by parallelism and/or repetition (*ll.* 39–81). The most elaborate parallelism is based on the anaphorically employed "not a," which recurs seven times and which is, because it is woven into subsidiary repetitions, spread over a total of fifteen lines. It is a pity in a way that, unlike his "pig-headed" poetic father, Walt Whitman, Pound did not use parallelism more often. We have to wait until we come to the "Pull down thy vanity" chant in Canto LXXXI to find something to match the skill Pound displays here, in arranging phrases and lines. Pound always accused people of having misunderstood what he meant by saying that the *Cantos* were rather like a fugue, not least because he did not think they knew what a fugue was. But if there are fugue-like blocks of lines, in addition to the fugal pattern which may exist on a grand scale, comprising whole Cantos and/or groups of Cantos, one such block is surely found in lines 32 to 56 of Canto IV.

It is not for nothing that Pound, in bringing together " 'Tis. 'Tis. Ytis!,"[14] "Actaeon" and the three words "and a valley," used the following spacing:

> 'Tis. 'Tis. Ytis!

> Actaeon...
>   and a valley (*ll.* 32−34).

The cry of the swallows, this typography implies, has not come to an end, but continues, is "sostenuto." The name "Actaeon," in the next line, is used as a one-word ellipsis, sufficient to alert those who remember the myth, and represents the first notes of the Vidal-Actaeon identity theme whose further development Pound decided to delay for another nineteen lines. But now, with the words "and a valley" a powerful third theme is intoned. To the cry of the swallows ("It is! It is!") Pound joins an equally insistent voice: "Not a ray, not a slivver, not a spare disc of sunlight" (*l.* 41). And into the midst of this bursts the song of a sister of the one the Germans have onomatopoeically called "die Lorelei," a siren whose beautiful singing becomes visualized in the beauty of her hair: surrounded by her nymphs, the great Diana, combing her hair, not golden like the Lorelei's, but "Ivory dipping in silver" (*ll.* 48 & 50), "Lifting, lifting and waffing" (*l.* 47). When the delayed Vidal-Actaeon identity theme joins in as well, all the voices, the cry of the swallows, the "Not a ray, not a slivver" chant, the irresistible "pale hair of the goddess" (*l.* 56) weld into one great revelation which, alas can last but "for a flash." Then comes the agony, the change to darkness.[15]

From syntactical parallelism to parallelism of theme. When Pound was once again explaining the design of the *Cantos,* in a letter to John Lackay Brown of April 1937, he finished with a comment on our Canto:

> There *is* at start, descent to the shades, metamorphosis, parallel (Vidal-Actaeon).[16]

No word about the two dozen other topics! Some twenty years after writing it Canto IV was to Pound simply this, "Parallel (Vidal-Actaeon)." Greek παρά meaning "alongside," plus Greek ἄλληλος meaning "one another." There is no denying, this is precisely what the two names are in line 52:

Then Actaeon: Vidal

a graphically indicated parallel. The word "parallel," in the sense of "comparison," "simile," was already in use in Shakespeare's time. We, as students of Pound, should be fascinated by this usage, since the word "parallel," can take us as close to the principle, as Pound saw it, of the Chinese written character as any English word can, always provided we see, immediately upon hearing it, two lines running in the same direction and of course keeping the same distance from each other. Two horizontal strokes on top of each other (Radical 7) have always signified "two" in Chinese picture writing. But then we can only use the number "two" if we have in front of us more than one thing of the same kind, if the two things are, if not identical, at least like each other, similar, or, as the character with the two horizontal strokes shows after all, parallel. So much for metaphor-making in ancient China and among the subjects of Elizabeth I, for whom geometry had gained new relevance through seafaring.

Let us now use the term "parallel" as a key to an understanding of the lines in which the names "Actaeon" and "Vidal" are alongside one another. For the moment we pretend that the two names are completely without history, the same as the letters A and V. What do we learn about A and V in lines 33 to 68, and about V in line 117 ("Vidal, or Ecbatan..."). They are not described, except for the fact that V is "old." And what are A and V doing? A seems to be doing nothing; he is merely leapt on: "The dogs leap on Actaeon" (*ll.* 57 & 63), but V is in fact said to be doing two things, "speaking" (*l.* 53), or "muttering, muttering Ovid" (*l.* 65) and "stumbling along in the wood" (*ll.* 54 & 64), and at least part of what he is muttering is recorded for us:

"Pergusa... pool... pool... Gargaphia,
"Pool... pool of Salmacis." (*ll.* 66—67)

Everything else is description, a polyphonic one, if we believe in the fugal structure of the passage, and there are no obvious connections between it and what is said about A and V. Fragmentary syntax is joined by fragmentary narrative. But does not a story stop being a story, if we do not get all of it? Of course, if the audience knows it already any bit of it will do. The only trouble is that no one is sure whether he has remembered the whole story, or even the right story. The picture of such confusion in the minds of the audience does not appear to have deterred Pound from making up his mind sometime before 1908, probably in the wake of Robert Browning, to abandon the telling of whole stories. He wrote to William Carlos Williams:

> To me the short so-called dramatic lyric—at any rate the sort of thing I do—is the poetic part of a drama the rest of which (to me the prose part) is left to the reader's imagination or implied or set in a short note. I catch the character I happen to be interested in at the moment he interests me, usually a moment of song, self-analysis, or sudden understanding or revelation. And the rest of the play would bore me and presumably the reader. I paint my man as I *conceive* him. Et voilà tout![17]

This really explains everything! The poem, in eleven six-line stanzas with one triple rhyme in each and a non-stanzaic ending, entitled "Piere Vidal Old," may just have been finished at the time, since it appeared in print within the year. Like some other poems about Provence it has indeed a note which puts the reader in the picture:

> It is of Piere Vidal, the fool *par excellence* of all Provence, of whom the tale tells how he ran mad, as a wolf, because of his love for Loba of Penautier, and how men hunted him with dogs through the mountains of Cabaret and brought him for dead to the dwelling of this Loba (she-wolf) of Penautier, and how she and her Lord had him healed and made welcome, and he stayed some time at that court. He speaks:

And then follows the persona, that is, old Vidal thinks out loud about "the great dead days," about having been as "swift as the king wolf...and as strong," a wolf known and feared among wolves, hinds and stags, but above all about his one night with Loba, a night, very significantly for Vidal's inclusion in the *Cantos,* "set deep in crystal."[18] In composing this mask Pound no doubt followed the strategy given at the beginning of the second part of "Near Perigord": "End fact. Try fiction."[19] If we read it together with the introductory note it is a fairly complete fiction. Hugh Witemeyer considers it possible that Arthur O'Shaughnessy's handling of the "man-to-wolf metamorphosis of Garulf Bisclavret," in a poem published in 1870, "might have helped Pound to pick out the mythic pattern in Vidal's adventure."[20] At any rate, by the time he was writing Cantos IV—VII, which are to Kenner "like a compendium of Pound's early poetry," and "a kaleidoscope of fancies, visions, glimpses, flickering wonders that merge into post-war unreality,"[21] Vidal, *conceived* by Pound out of the few known biographical facts and out of his own, in part rather daring, erotic imagination, was alongside Actaeon. Only Pound was no longer given to appending notes out of courtesy to the reader; he now "painted" his men without regard to comprehensibility, making poems like cubist *collages* in which many details are only decipherable, if you happen to have found those pieces which might have been used also, but were discarded in the heat of creation. If a pattern emerges you may gladly forget about the missing pieces, but what *exactly* is the "mythic pattern" existing in Vidal *and* Actaeon? How Vidal ought to be seen we can deduce reasonably clearly from the Vidal poem and from Pound's remarks on him in the chapter "Psychology and Troubadours" in *The Spirit of Romance*. Having emphasized that, like Dante's vision and like the poetry of Bertran de Born and Arnaut Marvoil, Vidal's verse "is real," because he ("that mad poseur Vidal"), like the rest of them, "lived it," and having quoted Vidal's "Good Lady, I think I see God when I gaze on your delicate body," he comments:

> You may take this if you like *cum grano*. Vidal was
> confessedly erratic. Still it is an obvious change from
> the manner of the Roman classics, and it cannot be
> regarded as a particularly pious or Christian expres-
> sion. If this state of mind was fostered by the writings
> of the early Christian fathers, we must regard their
> influence as purely indirect and unintentional
>   Richard St. Victor has left us one very beautiful
> passage on the splendours of paradise.
>   They are ineffable and innumerable and no man
> having beheld them can fittingly narrate them or even
> remember them exactly. Nevertheless by naming over
> all the most beautiful things we know we may draw
> back upon the mind some vestige of the heavenly
> splendour.[22]

If Richard St. Victor's "one beautiful passage" which
Pound mentions here included the sentence "UBI AMOR
IBI OCULUS EST," it now holds a very prominent place in
and at the end of Canto XC (606 & 609:640 & 643), in the
company of a whole galaxy of "other vestiges of heavenly
splendour." Unlike other figures appearing in the early
Cantos, including some from the three cancelled Ur-
Cantos, Vidal has no come-back in a later Canto. His name
is only "in the record" in Canto IV, the name of a fool who
was nevertheless "simplex naturae"[23] and helped to lead
Pound "back to splendour" (116/797:27).

Actaeon made his first appearance in 1915 when the
magazine *Poetry* published a "war poem" by Ezra Pound
entitled "The Coming of War: Actaeon," as mysterious and
haunting a poem as ever he wrote. Curiously enough, when
Pound recalled the figure of Actaeon in Pisa a phrase from
another poem of his, not from "The Coming of War" oc-
curred to him alongside the name:

> But for Actaeon
> of the eternal moods has fallen away (80/501:534).

The phrase "eternal moods" is from Δώρια, which evokes the same bleak seascape and landscape as "The Coming of War" and is equally mysterious:

> Be in me as the eternal moods
>   of the bleak wind, and not
> As transient things are—
>   gaiety of flowers.
> Have me in the strong loneliness
>   of sunless cliffs
> And of grey waters.
>   Let the gods speak softly of us
> In days hereafter,
>   The shadowy flowers of Orcus
> Remember thee.[24]

I do not think I can solve the mystery, but somehow the hunter Actaeon lived on as a spirit in nature, in Pound's imagination. The only link, however, between these two poems and Canto IV is the vision of gold. "Actaeon of golden greaves!" we read in "The Coming of War," and in line 60 of our Canto: "Gold, gold, a sheaf of hair." Years ago I suggested that the mention of gold might be said to evoke Pound's usury theme, gold as the cause of strife and mankind's common grave ("Aurum est commune sepulchrum. Usura commune sepulchrum").[25] However, this sheds no light on the nature of the parallel between Actaeon and Vidal. The one thing we can safely say, now that we know what Pound thought of Vidal and what sort of contexts he gave Actaeon, is that they both penetrated nature, became part of it and, like the speaker in the poem "The Tree," knew "the truth of things unseen before."[26] And we may gain further insight if we look at the "superpository image" which concludes the section:

> The empty armour shakes as the cygnet moves. (*l.* 68)

This is an adaptation of the lines in Ovid which give the end of the combat between Achilles and Cygnus the Invulnerable (*Met.* XII, 143–145). Pound may have superimposed this line, which renders the very moment of the death of the warrior and the birth of the swan, to suggest that what matters is not that one is hunted down or defeated, but that one perceives the beauty which, because it belongs to no life in particular, cannot die. The swan is the second species of bird in our Canto. Should we therefore see a "subject-rhyme" between the swallows and the swan?

Anyone who has studied Hugh Kenner's monumental book, *The Pound Era,* is thoroughly conditioned to the term "subject-rhyme," but it is so far not found in any dictionary. Since Kenner nowhere says that it was Pound himself who coined it, it is time someone did. As far as I can see, the word only occurs once in Pound's published work, in the letter to his father of 11 April, 1927. After outlining the fugal structure of the *Cantos,* he wrote:

> Various things keep cropping up in the poem. The original world of gods; the Trojan War, Helen on the wall of Troy with the old men fed up with the whole show and suggesting she be sent back to Greece.
>
> Rome founded by survivors of Troy. Here ref. to legendary founding of Este...
>
> Then in the delirium, Nicholo remembers or thinks he is watching death of Roland. Elvira on wall (subject-rhyme with Helen on Wall).[27]

The metaphoric use of the word "rhyme" is even older than the metaphoric use of "parallel," going right back to Chaucer's time, with the proverbial "neither rhyme nor reason" having its origin round about 1500. But in the combination with "subject" Pound really made it new. Wishing to take his father, to whom as to most people the *Cantos* were strange both in form and subject-matter, back to familiar ground, he hit upon "subject-rhyme," implying: You know what a rhyme is, Dad. Well, in the Cantos I do not repeat sounds like "love" and "dove," but I repeat similar subjects. In choosing "Elvira on the wall" as an example he at the same time indicated that such rhymes need not be alongside one another, but can be separated from each other by many Cantos. The "Helen on the wall of Troy" subject first occurs in Canto II, is recalled elliptically in Canto VII, in preparation, as it were, for the subject-rhyme, same situation but not the same people, in Canto XX.[28] Some critics would presumably speak of a recurrent *motif* here.

Kenner's use of the term, especially his saying that such and such "rhymes with," seems to have given rise to gentle mockery with some scholars.[29] But the claim Kenner makes for the concept of the "subject-rhyme" is indeed far-reaching:

> Pound's heuristic device is always the subject-rhyme. To elucidate the Italian New Birth of circa 1500, he compares it with the American of circa 1770. Specifically, Jefferson and his successors building a nation are rhymed with Malatesta building the Tempio, and a careful structural parallel enforces this rhyme.[30]

Having hinted that this tool, this, shall we say, telescope extending the eye of the voyaging explorer—how un-American of Pound never to have included Columbus in the *Cantos!*—which enables him to make out land long before any crewman's naked eye, this instrument the main quality of which must be its light-gathering power (Think of Kenner's fondness for "in the gloom the gold/Gathers the light about it" 17/78:82), so that the explorer never misses the "luminous detail" which he can match with a "luminous detail" already discovered and entered in the log-book; having hinted, then, that the concept of the subject-rhyme very probably came to Pound via Arnaut Daniel and his elaborate rhyming practice and via Gaudier and his defining "sculptural feeling" as "masses in relation," Kenner declares: "The *Cantos* affords a thesaurus of subject-rhymes."[31] What an image! But would it not be more in keeping with the humility of the old Pound to say that the *Cantos* only provide the notes towards such a thesaurus.

However, Kenner is not suggesting that it is all in the one book, and as far as he is concerned subject-rhyming frequently carries us from the *Cantos* to things outside them, which is as much as saying that "love" forms a rhyme with "dove" whether the word "dove" is part of a given poem or not. Of course, words do "rhyme," i.e. have associations with things that are not part of the structure of the poem they are in, but normally the question of relevance can be our guide. In the study of Pound's *Cantos,* however, it is often hard to know what is relevant and what is not.

How about things that do not rhyme? How does the poet who has abandoned most of the features of argumentative syntax, who gives mostly fragments which, however luminous, in the main merely "allude," but do not "present,"[32] make sure that we distinguish between what he condemns and what he approves; and is it possible for him to give shades in between? It lies in the very nature of "subject-rhyming" that good can only rhyme with good and bad with bad, but never good with bad. Ultimately everything bad in Pound's *Cantos* and his other works rhymes with usury or greed, and destruction, and everything good with fine work, beauty, splendour. Yet there are details in the *Cantos* about which the reader cannot make up his mind, because he lacks the key to them. Forced into a decision he is liable to take the wrong one. Daniel Pearlman thinks that "Ecbatan of plotted streets" (*l.* 101) in our Canto is "a city of injustice," whereas I took it to be an image or an anticipation of the Ideal City. I am unable to determine who is right, he or I.[33] In other words, subject-rhymes do not help me to find contrasts and the subtle differences between the things rhymed. They do not tell me what I should think, for example, of Polhonac, or Gyges, although they rhyme, since they are in juxtapostion with them, with Cabestan and Terreus.

Since I have dealt with such minutiae elsewhere,[34] and since I hope I have said enough about the microstructures of Canto IV, I pass on to the most important question, that of the overall structural unity. Canto IV has no obvious unifying features, no unbroken story-line, no easy to follow, well-ordered argument. Thinking of the Canto as a drama we can say that none of the three unities is observed; the human drama is broken up into disconnected scenes. The time span covered is that from the fall of Troy to the time after World War I, so that the opening image of ruins may be regarded as evoking the sad outcome of both. But the span of roughly 3000 years is unimportant as time. The time span that matters is the one that no war, no human folly can destroy, as long as nature exists: it is the single day, every day, the day as portent that after every period of darkness there is a new period of light. The proof that Canto IV has this message is for me in the three nature lyrics, what I have called the Dawn Lyric, the Noon Lyric and the Evening Lyric. These three lyrics tell us that the cosmos continues even after a war. All the stories evoked or alluded to cluster round the three lyrics. They are not strictly assigned to any particular time of day, except for the Vidal-Actaeon parallel which requires the midday sun for its enactment. The Noon Lyric is, as it were, an attempt to tackle the ineffable, a "naming over [of] all the most beautiful things" Pound knew at the time of writing Canto IV. With Arnaut Daniel's vision of the raining sunlight ("e lo soleils plovil" [*l.* 69]), the trees embodying conjugal virtue (the Japanese equivalent of Philemon and Baucis), the world of the Noh plays generally and the crystal sea full of gods it is indubitably the "emotional still centre" of Canto IV, anticipating Canto XLIX, where Hugh Kenner has discovered the "still centre" of the whole poem, and preparing the reader for the crystal visions of the post-Pisan Cantos.

Whereas the Canto has a definite point of departure, the ruins of a civilization, it has no fixed ending. "And we sit here.../there in the arena..." at the end can only mean that the drama continues, the tragedy caused, not by nature, but by man himself. Yet the contemplation of spiritual experiences of figures like Vidal or Actaeon has nevertheless given rise to a belief in the unbelievable, in the rebirth of love and beauty out of the rubble heap, where love becomes the eye that sees the beauty. As Eugene Paul Nassar, who advocates a strictly dualistic view of Pound, says very aptly: "The *Cantos*, early and late, have been variations on the light in the darkness: the light affirmed, the darkness never denied."[35] And now we can answer the question as to whether the birds in Canto IV "rhyme" in any particular way. With their tragic origins the swallows and the swan not only rhyme with each other and with all the other birds in the *Cantos*, the birds in Janequin's "Chant des Oiseaux," the birds in Pisa, Whitman's widowed mockingbird and the "white-chested martin" whom Pound made a messenger of love, but also with rebirth, with light out of darkness, with splendour out of despair.

Notes

Homberger: Modernists and Edwardians

1. This review is reprinted in Eric Homberger, ed., *Ezra Pound: The Critical Heritage* (London and Boston: Routledge & Kegan Paul, 1972), pp. 55–57.
2. T. S. Eliot, *To Criticize the Critic and other writings* (London: Faber & Faber, 1965), p. 189.
3. Arnold Bennett to George Sturt, 8 March 1896, *Letters of Arnold Bennett*, ed. James Hepburn (London: Oxford University Press, 1968), II, p. 38.
4. Christopher Hassall, *Edward Marsh, Patron of the Arts* (London: Longmans, 1959), p. 523.
5. Pound to Harriet Monroe, ? September 1913, *The Letters of Ezra Pound 1907–1941*, ed. D. D. Paige (London: Faber & Faber, 1951), p. 60. But see the letter of 7 November 1913 to Miss Monroe, where Pound says that it is not only an awareness of Paris which will help Chicago "slough off its provincialism", but of the value of any metropolis other than London.
6. See Eric Homberger, "A Study of Ezra Pound's Poetry and Aesthetic from 1908 to 1920, with special reference to his view of the Poet's Social Responsibility" (Ph.D. diss., Cambridge University, 1971), chs. 2–3.

Makin: Pound's Provence and the Medieval Paideuma

1. Ezra Pound, *Guide to Kulchur*, (London, 1966), p. 57.
2. These matters are discussed in a book on Pound's

Provence that I am currently completing.

3. Cf. e.g. 91/610:644 (i.e. Ezra Pound, *The Cantos of Ezra Pound,* (London, 1975), p. 610; id. *The Cantos of Ezra Pound,* (London, 1964), p. 644 (Canto XCI). Since the pagination of the London 1975 edition is as that of the New York 1970 edition, this method of numbering follows that elaborated by Hugh Kenner for *The Pound Era;* I use it throughout here.

4. Cf. Peter Makin, "Ezra Pound and Scotus Erigena," *Comparative Literature Studies* X.1 (March 1973) esp. pp. 73–77. Cf. also James J. Wilhelm "In Praise of Anselm: An Approach to Canto 105," *Paideuma* 2.3 (Winter 1973), esp. pp. 399–402.

5. Ezra Pound *The Selected Letters of Ezra Pound 1907–1941,* ed. D. D. Paige, (N.Y., 1971), p. 335 (to T. S. Eliot, 18 Jan. 1940).

6. Ezra Pound, "Psychology and Troubadours," *Quest* IV.1 (Oct. 1912) pp. 37–53, esp. pp. 51–53. Pound cites six lines from the *Jesu corona virginum* of St. Ambrose, taken (with Gourmont's omissions) from Remy de Gourmont *Le Latin mystique,* (Paris, 1930), p. 55. He says that they are from "Hymns to Christ," a strange reference, as is that for his quotation from the Mozarabic liturgy on the same page (p. 104 in Gourmont): "From 'Ode on St. Colum.' " When on the following page he quotes at length from Gottschalk of Limburg, he mistakenly takes two pieces quoted separately in Gourmont (pp. 143–144) as part of the same sequence, and instead of calling them a "sequence" he entitles them "sequaire," which must be misread from Gourmont's running title "Les séquentiaires," "the sequence-writers." These things show how dependent Pound was on Gourmont for his knowledge of mediaeval Christian Latin poetry. It is true that periods are clearly distinguished from each other in Gourmont, but Pound probably noted down rapidly the lines that interested him as he read them, and took

them for parts of the same chronological lump when he referred back to them.

7. Reprinted in Ezra Pound, *Literary Essays of Ezra Pound,* ed. T. S. Eliot, (London, 1960), pp. 339–358.
8. Gourmont, *Le Latin mystique,* pp. 277–278. All translations are mine unless I note otherwise.
9. *Ibid.,* p. 330.
10. *Ibid.,* pp. 178–179
11. *Ibid.,* p. 333.
12. *Ibid.,* p. 335; pp. 337–338.
13. *Ibid.,* pp. 339–340.
14. Cf. esp. ibid., pp. 394–397, "Formation du bréviaire romain actuel."
15. *Ibid.,* pp. 270, 297, 353, 385.
16. *Ibid.,* p. 345.
17. *Ibid.,* p. 342; cf. p. 163, on the litanies:
    > . . .en devenant de bibliques chrétiennes, elles ajoutent l'amour à l'adoration, à la supplication les larmes, à l'abandon vers l'absolu pouvoir, l'espoir en la mansuétude de Jésus souffrant.
18. *Ibid.,* pp. 261, 384. Symbolist writers are peppered here and there as standards of comparison, perhaps intended to make Gourmont's readers feel that the Latin poets are something that their own sensibilities too can accommodate; cf. pp. 22, 327. Sometimes the conjunctions shed a strange light on Gourmont's aesthetics, as when he speaks of "Catulle, ce Verlaine" (p. 22).
19. The most impressive peroration in the book is this, describing a fifteenth-century terracotta of the Virgin and Child (p. 378):
    > She does not weep: she is transfixed by terror. She sees. Her whole face bears the terrifying stigmata of the painful hallucination. The fixed eye is terrified by the apparition that cannot be denied. In this eye there are the agony in the garden, the betrayal by Judas, the denial by Peter, the whipping at the cross, the spitting, the cross dragged like a chain the length

> of Golgotha, the hands pierced by the nails, the
> blood that flows through the screen of the ironic
> thorns and blinds the eyes...

20. Remy de Gourmont, *Lettres à l'Amazone*, (Paris, 1922), p. 282.

21. Pound, *Literary Essays*, p. 340.

22. Cf. esp. Gourmont, *Le Latin mystique*, p. 27.

23. *Ibid.*, p. 21.

24. *Ibid.*, p. 27:

> ...what signs of decadence can one see in this poem
> worked by a grieving *(douloureuse)* but sure hand, on
> very noble lines, of veils stiffened by tears of blood,
> in this mourning-robe that is fringed with green
> gold, studded with amethysts?

    Cf. also pp. 226–227 on jewels. In Gourmont's basic opposition of "official/orderly/stupid" to "private/wild/sensitive," classical Rome belongs to the former, while mediaeval Latin is helped towards the latter by an influence from barbaric Orientals (cf. esp. p. 21). See also the "amour désordonné du verbe" of the " musiciens barbares" after Godeschalk (p. 23).

25. Cf. esp. Wilhelm, "In Praise of Anselm," p. 404 on not wanting " 'to bust out of the kosmos', an 'accensio' (kindling; but better perhaps *ascensio*, lofty flight) that is impossible since, according to Anselm, the cosmos includes not only us but all that is."

26. Pound, "Psychology and Troubadours," p. 50.

27. *Ibid.*, p. 46.

28. Gourmont, *Le Latin mystique*, p. 255.

29. Pound, "Psychology and Troubadours," p. 51 and note. It is possible that Pound's ignoring of all marks showing omission in Gourmont comes from having made hasty notes in the British Museum or from books borrowed from F. S. Flint.

30. *Cant.* ii. 16 "qui pascitur inter lilia," cf. vi. 3; i. 3 "post te curremus"; ii. 6 "Fulcite me floribus, stipate me malis": Migne, *Patrologia Latina*, XXVIII, cols. 1352–1356. For

a text of the *Jesu corona virginum* see A. S. Walpole, *Early Latin Hymns,* (Cambridge, 1922), pp. 112–113. The *Nardus Columbae floruit,* of which Gourmont quotes one stanza (*Le Latin mystique,* p. 104), is in the second part of the Mozarabic liturgy, Migne, *Patrologia Latina,* LXXXVI col. 1310. Pound's "encompass her with apple-boughs" follows Gourmont in taking *malis* to be *malus* "apple-tree" rather than *malum* "apple"; contrast the Authorised Version's "comfort me with apples."

31. 16/69:73.
32. 21/96:103–104.
33. Ezra Pound, *Selected Poems,* ed. T. S. Eliot, (London, 1959), pp. 98–99 (publ. Apr. 1913: Gallup C76).
34. *Cant.* vii. 4–7, in Migne, *Patrologia Latina,* XXVIII col. 1356.
35. *Cant.* vii. 2–4.
36. 29/145:150 (publ. Apr./June 1930: Gallup C764). For the phallic stiffness see " 'God what a woman! / My God what a woman' said the King telo rigido," 20/91:95.
37. Pound, "Psychology and Troubadours," p. 48.
38. Pound, *Literary Essays,* p. 151; "Psychology and Troubadours," p. 50. See also ibid., p. 50, saying that the attitudes of Ovid and of Arnaut Daniel "are notably different, as for instance on such a matter as delay. Ovid takes no account of the psychic function."
39. Ed. Walpole, *Early Latin Hymns,* pp. 112–113; my trans.
40. For a hint of the tradition see Dom Cuthbert Butler, *Western Mysticism,* (London, 1967), p. 97.
41. Cf. ed. Walpole, *Early Latin Hymns,* p. 114 quoting Ambrose *in Ps.* XXXVII.53 on the "wounds" of sin "ut puta iniustitiae, intemperantiae, inpudicitiae."
42. Cf. Thaddeus Zielinski, *The Religion of Ancient Greece: An Outline,* (London, 1926), pp. 17 ff.; Ezra Pound, *Gold and Labour,* (London, 1951), pp. 3–4.
43. Cf. 39/195:203; the "pale foot alternate" is from 4/13:17.

44. Cf. above, note 30.

45. "Religio," *Townsman* II.8 (Nov. 1939), p. 4. Cf. e.g. 74/435:462: "in coitu inluminatio."

46. Pound, "Psychology and Troubadours," p. 51. The *Victimae paschali* sequence, "ascribed to Wipo (d. 1050), chaplain to the Emperors Conrad II and Henry III" (F. J. E. Raby, *The Poetry of the Eucharist,* (London, 1957), p. 16) is quoted in full in Gourmont, *Le Latin mystique,* p. 147, where Pound presumably found it. For a text see Raby, *loc. cit.,* or G. M. Dreves, *Ein Jahrtausend Lateinischer Hymnendichtung,* (Leipzig, 1909), I, pp. 147–148.

47. Pound, "Psychology and Troubadours," p. 52; cf. above, note 6; Gourmont, *Le Latin mystique,* p. 144. Gourmont's text follows ed. Joseph Kehrein, *Lateinische Sequenzen des Mittelalters,* (Mainz, 1873), pp. 333–334, with omissions shown and with changes of punctuation. Pound's "placing his head" translates the Latin "collocans cubiculum," "placing his bed" (Gourmont only has "il se couche"). Pound's "virginal retreats" for "Virginales... recessus," where Gourmont has "girons virginaux," also suggests that he was working from the Latin cited by Gourmont, rather than from Gourmont's translations.

48. Cf. ed. Kehrein, *Lateinische Sequenzen,* p. 334 note.

49. Contrast Ambrose's treatment of the Virgin Birth, straightforward and yet not insensitive, in ed. Walpole, *Early Latin Hymns,* pp. 53–54:

> non ex uirile semine,
> sed mystico spiramine
> Verbum Dei factum est caro,
> fructusque ventris floruit.
>
> aluus tumescit uirginis,
> claustrum pudoris permanet,
> uexilla uirtutum micant,
> uersatur in templo Deus.

50. Cf. Migne, *Patrologia Latina,* CXLI, col. 1326 note.

51. Cf. esp. *ibid:*

> 9. Murmurat Pharisaeus, ubi plorat femina criminis conscia...
> 11. Pedes amplectitur Dominicos, lacrymis lavat, tergit crinibus, lavando, tergendo, unguento unxit, osculis circuit.

52. Pound, *Selected Letters,* p. 335 (to T. S. Eliot, 18 Jan. 1940). For the "sequaire" see above, note 6.
53. Pound, "Psychology and Troubadours," pp. 52–53.
54. Pound, "Deus est amor," *Townsman* III. 11 (June 1940), p. 14.
55. Pound, *Selected Prose,* ed. William Cookson, (London, 1973), p. 57, publ. 1931–32 (Gallup C840).
56. Cf. Gerson, quoted by Gourmont in *Le Latin mystique,* p. 337:

> "There is nothing more suspect than love, even towards God"; and Gerson adds: "Especially in women or in men with a feminine temperament—*viros muliebriter complexionatos.*" ... the mystery that is most charged with meditations is the one that alone abundantly evokes images of a certain sweetness.

One should mention a more enduring (though slight) debt to Gottschalk of Limburg and to Gourmont. Contrasting the Pharisee's reaction to Mary Magdalen with Christ's, the second sequence says:

> The sinner despises his fellow-sinner; you, knowing no sin, hearken to the penitent, clean the soiled woman, love in order that you may make her beautiful.

Gourmont comments (p. 143): " 'You love her so that she may be beautiful,—Amas ut pulchram facias',—O noble mind, so advanced in idealism." In the 1920 essay, at a time when Pound's thought was far more mature, he remarked of Gourmont that

> The study of emotion does not follow a set chronological arc: it extends from the *Physique de l'Amour* to *Le Latin Mystique;* from the condensation

of Fabre's knowledge of insects to
   Amas ut facias pulchram
  in the Sequaire of Goddeschalk...

(Literary Essays, p. 341). This suggests a relation between lover and beloved the exact reverse of that in the Propertius so frequently quoted by Pound, both in discussing Gourmont and elsewhere:

Ingenium nobis ipsa puella fecit

translated by Pound as

My genius is no more than a girl

However, in both cases, love creates the personality. In both cases also, I think, Pound concluded that the thought was a stray one, of great interest in itself but not really belonging with the sensibility that produced it (cf. *Literary Essays,* p. 151 on Propertius). I believe he never returned to Gottschalk.

57. Pound, *Literary Essays,* pp. 149−155, publ. 1928: Gallup C710; Pound, *Selected Prose,* ed. Cookson, pp. 54−60.
58. Pound, *Selected Prose,* ed. Cookson p. 53, publ. 1930: Gallup C792; Pound, *Literary Essays,* p. 151, publ. 1928: Gallup C710.
59. Ezra Pound, *The Spirit of Romance,* (NY, 1968) p. 31, publ. 1910: Gallup A5.
60. Arnaut Daniel, *Canzoni,* ed. Gianluigi Toja, (Florence, 1960), p. 337; Bernard de Ventadour, *Chansons d'Amour,* ed. Moshé Lazar, (Frankfurt/Paris, 1966), p. 232.
61. *Ibid.,* p. 136.
62. Pound, *Selected Prose,* ed. Cookson, p. 58.
63. Pound, *Guide to Kulchur,* pp. 294−295, cf. 36/179:185; Pound, *Selected Prose,* ed. Cookson p. 52.
64. Ezra Pound, *A Visiting Card,* tr. John Drummond, (London, 1952), p. 7 (publ. as *Carta da Visita* in 1942: Gallup A50).

65. Butler, *Western Mysticism,* p. 96.
66. Migne, *Patrologia Latina,* CLXXIV, col. 1307, part of which is quoted by Gourmont in *Le Latin mystique,* p. 247.
67. Migne, *Patrologia Latina,* CLXXXIV, col. 1316 (cf. Gourmont, *Le Latin mystique,* p. 248).
68. Cf. Migne, *Patrologia Latina,* CLXXIV, col. 1310; ibid. col. 1308. Cf. the *Garden of Delights* of the Abbess of Hohenburg, noted by Gourmont in *Le Latin mystique,* p. 252, where we are warned that after death

> It is said that a man's marrow turns into snakes and his brain into toads...

69. Migne, *Patrologia Latina,* CLXXXIV, col. 753 ff.
70. In the third Sermon, having established the "kiss of his mouth" of the *Canticle* as the divine union, and the "Nigra... sed formosa" as the cleansed sinner, Bernard introduces another kiss, of his own invention: first, one must prostrate oneself and kiss the divine feet. Then, he says, one cannot go straight from feet to mouth:

> It is a long and formidable jump from the foot to the mouth, a manner of approach that is not commendable.

So one must go via another Bernard-introduced stage, the hand. Of course, all these are only metaphors for progress towards the divine union. But the logic of the thing is sustained by the *physical* term of the metaphor, without which of course it would be redundant: you cannot kiss the deity on the lips while your face is all muddy, etc. It is obvious that Bernard ignores all the inner consistency of the world (that of the *Canticle*) from which he takes the metaphors; he then proceeds to ignore any consistency that might be built up with his own extensions of these metaphors, throwing in new metaphors, and emphasising the physical or the theological term according to the needs of his argument. Imagery cannot be treated in this way without either becoming completely weakened or getting out of control; in either case it makes a bad poem. See Bernard of Clairvaux, *The Works of Bernard of Clairvaux*, vol. 2: *On the Song of Songs I*, tr. Kilian Walsh OCSO, (Shannon, 1971), pp. 17–19 (Migne, *Patrologia Latina*, CLXXXIII, cols. 794–795).

71. Cf. ed. Walter L. Wakefield and Austin P. Evans, *Heresies of the High Middle Ages*, (NY and London, 1969), p. 123 (from Migne, *Patrologia Latina*, CLXXXII, col. 434), where Bernard claims that Henry would deny baptism to children, thus denying them the Christian life:

> Is it from innocents alone, then, that God, who has saved both men and beasts as He has multiplied His mercies, withholds that same overflowing mercy? Why, I ask, why does this man begrudge to children the child Savior who was born to them? This is diabolical jealousy! Because of it, death has entered the world. Or does the man assume that children need no savior because they are children? If that is so, then for naught did the Mighty Lord become a little child, not to mention that He was scourged, was spat upon, was crucified, and finally died.

72. Dreves, *Ein Jahrtausend Lateinischer Hymnendichtung*, II, p. 17. Kehrein, *Lateinische Sequenzen des Mittelalters*, p. 31, notes that his anthology contains twelve imitations of this.

73. Gourmont, *Le Latin mystique*, p. 254; cf. ed. Henry Spitzmuller, *Poésie latine chrétienne du Moyen âge*, (Bruges, 1971), pp. 558–561.

74. Dreves, *Ein Jahrtausend Lateinischer Hymnendichtung*, II, pp. 35–36.

75. Gourmont, *Le Latin mystique*, pp. 249, 247. Gourmont follows Migne, *Patrologia Latina*, CLXXXIV, cols. 1313-1316, cutting out several stanzas without (at least in my edition) any indication. Preferring, as scholars will, to attribute irregularity rather to lunacy or accident than to aesthetic purpose, J. B. Hauréau in *Des*

poèmes latins attribués à Saint Bernard, (Paris, 1890), p. 25, considers that there are in fact two separate poems in this piece. If so, I would argue that the paster-together was a man of genius. For a text omitting the 'Dic ubi Salomon...' see Dreves *Ein Jahrtausend Lateinischer Hymnendichtung,* II, pp. 453–454. The stanzas that I have quoted may be translated thus:

> Whoever thinks of death, I marvel that he is happy:
> as the race of men is thus allotted to death,
> whither man may go after death is unknown:
> Wherefore a certain sage speaks thus: [...]

> Say where is Solomon, once so noble,
> or where Samson, the invincible leader?
> or the more beautiful Absalom, marvellous of face?
> or the sweet and desirable Jonathan?

76. Quoted by Gourmont in *Le Latin mystique,* p. 31:

> ... Clara facies satis est et forma venusta
> Et tibi non minimum lactea tota placet.
> Viscera si pateant occulta et caeteris carnis
> Carnes quas sordes contegat alba cutis!...

77. Cf. esp. Pound, *Selected Prose,* ed. Cookson, pp. 58–59.

78. Cf. Hauréau, *Des poèmes latins attribués à Saint Bernard,* p. 60; ed. F. J. E. Raby, *The Oxford Book of Medieval Latin Verse,* (Oxford, 1959), p. 493 (note to no. 233), citing ed. A. Wilmart, *Le "Jubilus" dit de Saint Bernard,* (Rome, 1944). The claim of Hauréau that Bernard wrote none of the verse ascribed to him has been disputed, and the aesthetic considerations that enter into his argument (e.g. pp. 64–66) are weakened by his obvious blindness to all the beauties of these works (pp. 24, 26, and esp. 66 and 97–98, where he forgives Saint Bernard for not liking Aristotle and Plato, but still thinks he should be spared having the products of these "plats rimailleurs," the hymn-writers, laid at his door).

79. We cannot ultimately do without some belief in historical connection; unless we believe that, for example,

"There was or could have been (given prevailing conditions) a congeries called Sigismondo Malatesta, in which X tendency coexisted with Y," which is an historical assertion, there is no basis for consideration of human possibilities and limitations. But the connections between human tendencies are much more "visible" and less fallible in poetry or painting than in argumentative prose.

80. Pound, *Literary Essays*, p. 154 ("Mediaevalism").
81. Pound, *Guide to Kulchur,* p. 144.
82. Ed. Walpole, *Early Latin Hymns,* p. 229:

> Fulgentis auctor aetheris,
> qui lunam lumen noctibus,
> solem dierum cursibus
> certo fundasti tramite;
>
> nox atra iam depellitur,
> mundi nitor renascitur,
> nouusque iam mentis uigor
> dulces in actus erigit.

Cf. esp. *ibid.* p. 35 (Ambrose, *Splendor paternae gloriae*), p. 224 (anon., *Lucis largitor splendide*), etc.

83. Cf. e.g. *ibid.* pp. 54−56 (Ambrose, *Intende, qui regis Israel*),

> where Christ
> procedat e thalamo suo,
> pudoris aula regia,
> geminae gigas substantiae;
> alacris occurrat viam...
>
> praesepe iam fulget tuum
> lumenque nox spirat nouum,
> quod nulla nox interpolet
> fideque iugi luceat.

The first line is from *Psalms,* xix.5, where it refers to the sun. Cf. also Notker's sequence *De Nativitate Domini,* cited in Gourmont, *Le Latin mystique,* p. 133; and the *Laetabundus,* quoted at length above, etc.

84. Cf. Ezra Pound, *Make It New,* (London, 1934), p. 173.

85. Pound, *Selected Prose*, ed. Cookson, p. 58 ("Terra Italica").
86. Dreves, *Ein Jahrtausend Lateinischer Hymnendichtung*, I, p. 392; cf. Jacopone da Todi, *Laude*, ed. Franco Mancini, (Rome/Bari, 1974), p. 339, and on the authorship, pp. 454–456. Cf. also the closely-related *Recordare sanctae crucis* of St. Bonaventure, in Dreves, *Ein Jahrtausend Lateinischer Hymnendichtung*, I, pp. 351–354:

> Christo sis confixus cruci,
> Ut tu valeas perduci
>   Secum ad caelestia.
>
> Quaere crucem, quaere clavos,
> Quaere manus, pedes cavos,
>   Quaere fossam lateris...
>
> Crucifixi, fac me fortem,
> Ut libenter tuam mortem
>   Plangam, donec vixero,
> Tecum volo vulnerari,
> Te libenter amplexari
>   In cruce desidero.
>
> Da cruorem quasi rorem,
> Ut te plorem, redemptorem
>   Christum, qui me refoves;
> Non te trices, sed felices
> Cicatrices mille vices
>   Tuas in me renoves.

Though, as we have seen, Pound in 1912 welcomed the "personality" of Christ in Gottschalk's writings, he would probably later have regretted the shift from the earlier Latin hymns, full of delight in the natural cycles, to this personal attention to the suffering Christ.

87. *Ibid.*, I, pp. 329–330.
88. Ezra Pound, "Deus est amor," *Townsman*, III.11 (June 1940), p. 14.
89. The drift of much writing about St. Francis since the modern revival of interest in him is that one should

dismiss all later developments of Franciscanism because they are not what St. Francis intended. A parallel
phenomenon might be the relatively new interest
among Japanese Buddhists in the Indian origins of
their religion, which could threaten to throw away the
whole Japanese-Chinese development of it in favour of
what "came first."

90. Ezra Pound, *Impact*, ed. Noel Stock, (Chicago, 1960), p.
200. This 1959 note seems to raise a problem Pound
had not been aware of until then, and which he did not
go on to solve. But as a swerve towards Eliot's emphasis
on orthodoxy (continuity of group heritage) and a re-
laxation of Pound's aesthetics-based eclecticism, it may
have been influenced by a need he felt at that moment
to earn Eliot's moral support in a time of great self-
doubt; see C. David Heyman *Ezra Pound: The Last
Rower*, New York 1976, pp. 268–269. Cf. Pound,
"Deus est amor," p. 14, where the point is perhaps
compromised by saying that the *race* must create its own
gods.

91. Pound, *The Spirit of Romance*, p. 101. I have not iden-
tified the text that Pound used (cf. his remarks on p.
103); "blanca luna" and "vaghe stelle" are not among
the variants mentioned by Vittore Branca in *Il Cantico
di Frate Sole: Studio delle Fonti e Testo Critico*, (Florence,
1950), p. 84. Cf. Paul Sabatier, *Vie de S. François d'Assise*,
(Paris, 1894), p. 349.

92. Ed. Ezra Pound and Marcella Spann, *Confucius to
Cummings*, (N.Y., 1964), pp. 86–88; though the two
rammed-together pieces of Gottschalk, still entitled
"Sequaire" and this time attributed to the Gottschalk
who lived in Scotus Erigena's time, are also reprinted,
ibid., pp. 75–76. The *In foco amor mi mise*, not now
included by scholars among St. Francis's writings (cf.
John R. H. Moorman, *The Sources for the Life of S. Francis
of Assisi*, [Manchester, 1940], p. 13), appears in the Cantos (20/92–93:97), though in such a context as to bring

out its somewhat Swinburnian qualities of narcissistic
adoration. Pound may have remembered it from
Gourmont, *Le Latin mystique,* pp. 258–259, though the
text differs.

93. Pound, *Guide to Kulchur,* pp. 141–142.

94. Pound, *Selected Prose,* p. 62 ("Ecclesiastical History,"
publ. 1934: Gallup C1083), quoting a friend. It is true
that sections of the followers of St. Francis almost immediately went over into fanatic asceticism, and the
Fraticelli, Minimi or Spiritual Franciscans were ex-
communicated for their excesses in that direction.
They have been associated with the alleged dualism of
the Cathars of Languedoc and North Italy. The *Dies
Irae* and the *Stabat Mater* (cf. above, notes 86, 87) are
Franciscan poems in that they are attributed to the
Franciscan monks Thomas of Celano and Jacopone da
Todi, who died in 1250 and 1306 respectively, not so
long after St. Francis's own death in 1226. All this
shows what a tremendous gap in aesthetics may exist
between groups of people that another age would tend
to lump together, and the great danger of arguing by
association.

95. Cf. Moorman, *The Sources for the Life of S. Francis,* p. 21.

96. Cf. *ibid.,* p. 29: "Brothers, brothers; the Lord hath
called me by the way of humility, and He has shown me
the way of simplicity; and I do not want you to mention
to me any other Rule, neither that of S. Augustine, nor
of S. Benedict, nor of S. Bernard. And the Lord told me
that He wished me to be a new fool in the world and
that He did not want to lead us by any other way than by
that wisdom; for by our learning and your wisdom God
will confound you." Here learning is clearly connected
with institutionalisation. Hence also St. Francis's insis-
tence in the Testament that his precepts should not be
commented on (cf. ed. Heinrich Boehmer, *Analekten
zur Geschichte des Franciscus von Assisi,* [Tübingen, 1930],
p. 27). His fears were well founded: when the brothers

began to study, it was for the purpose of combatting heresy (cf. Moorman, *Sources for the Life of S. Francis,* p. 86).

97. Cf. *ibid.,* p. 124. The ambiguity of the Testament in regard to the priesthood almost amounts to "Father, forgive them; for they know not what they do" (cf. ed. Boehmer, *Analekten zur Geschichte des Franciscus,* p. 25), but St. Francis could no more wish to abolish priests than Christ wished to abolish mankind.

98. For the following see Raffaello Morghen, *Francescanesimo e Rinascimento* in *Convegni del Centro di Studi sulla Spiritualita medievale I: Jacopone e il suo Tempo, 13 –15 ottobre 1957,* Todi 1959, pp. 13–36, esp. pp. 27–28, 21–22, 14 (quoting Salvatorelli), 16–17, 22, 28–29, 30, 33–34.

Monk: Pound's Use of Translation

1. "Vorticism," *Fortnightly Review* (Sept. 1914), reprinted in *Gaudier-Brzeska: A Memoir* (1916), p. 106.
2. "I gather the Limbs of Osiris," *Selected Prose* (ed. Cookson), p. 34.
3. "How to Read," *Literary Essays of Ezra Pound* (ed. Eliot), p. 16.
4. "Troubadors—their Sorts and Conditions," *Literary Essays,* p. 101.
5. *Antheil and the Treatise on Harmony,* (Da Capo, 1968), p. 123.
6. "How to Read," *Literary Essays,* p. 25.
7. *Ibid.,* p. 25.
8. "I gather the Limbs of Osiris," *Selected Prose,* p. 27.
9. *Ibid.,* p. 33.
10. *Ibid.,* p. 33.
11. *Ibid.,* p. 43.
12. To W. H. D. Rouse, February 1935, *The Letters of Ezra Pound (1907 –41),* (ed. Paige), p. 269.
13. "Early Translators of Homer," *Literary Essays,* p. 273.

14. "Notes on Elizabethan Classicists," *Literary Essays*, p. 247.
15. To W.H.D. Rouse, April 1935, *Letters*, p. 273.
16. "Notes on Elizabethan Classicists," p. 238 *n*.
17. "How to Read," *Literary Essays*, p. 35.
18. "Early Translators of Homer," *Literary Essays*, p. 249.
19. "Arnaut Daniel," *Literary Essays*, p. 109.
20. *ABC of Reading*, p. 51.
21. "How to Read," *Literary Essays*, p. 25.
22. To Katue Kitasono, 11 March 1937, *Letters*, p. 293.
23. To Katue Kitasono, 15 November 1940, *Letters*, p. 347.
24. "How to Read," *Literary Essays*, p. 25.
25. To John Drummond, 18 February 1932, *Letters*, p. 239.
26. To Thomas Hardy, February 1921 (?), quot. *Southern Review* (Winter, 1968).
27. To A. R. Orage, April 1919, *Letters*, p. 150.
28. To Thomas Hardy, 31 March 1921, *op. cit.*
29. Donald Davie, *Pound*, (Fontana, 1975), p. 61.
30. "What I feel about Walt Whitman," *Selected Prose*, p. 115.
31. *Ibid.*, p. 116.
32. "I gather the Limbs of Osiris," *Selected Prose*, p. 32.
33. *Ibid.*, p. 33.

Bell: Mauberley's Barrier of Style

1. The best work is to be found in the standard commentaries: Hugh Kenner, *The Poetry of Ezra Pound*, (New York, 1950), pp. 164–182; John J. Espey, *Ezra Pound's Mauberley, A Study in Composition*, London 1955; G. S. Fraser, *Ezra Pound* ("Writers and Critics" series, London, 1960), pp. 52–63; M. L. Rosenthal, *A Primer of Ezra Pound*, (New York, 1960), pp. 29–41; Donald Davie, "Ezra Pound's *Hugh Selwyn Mauberley*" in *The Pelican Guide to English Literature*, Vol. VII (1961), 2nd ed., London, 1963, pp. 315–329, and *Poet as Sculptor*, London, 1965, pp. 91–101; William V. Spanos, "The

Modulating Voice of Hugh Selwyn Mauberley," *Wisconsin Studies in Contemporary Literature*, VI. 1 (Winter–Spring, 1965), pp. 73–96; Hugh Witemeyer, *The Poetry of Ezra Pound. Forms and Renewal 1908–1920*, (Berkeley, 1969), pp. 161–195; K. K. Ruthven, *A Guide to Ezra Pound's Personae (1926)*, Berkeley, 1969), pp. 126–147.

 The most detailed commentary on the poem is Jo Brantley Berryman, *Ezra Pound Versus Hugh Selwyn Mauberly: A Distinction*, unpublished Ph.D. theses, University of Southern California, 1973. Part of the thesis has emerged in print as " 'Medallion': Pound's Poem," *Paideuma*, II. 3 (Winter 1973), pp. 391–398.

2. Pound defined the "impressionist" once and for all in a famous statement of 1913: "An impressionist is one who does not seek to impress us. An impressionist cares little either about us or himself. He is neither pleased nor displeased with his subject. He is mildly pleased to be conscious." (*New Freewoman*, I. 12 [1 December 1913], p. 227). Needless to say, I cannot see such a definition as in any way applicable to Mauberley's activity.

3. Paul Elmer More, "The Quest of a Century," *Shelburne Essays*, Vol. III (1905), (Phaeton Press ed., London, 1967), pp. 244–265.

4. The major exception being G. S. Fraser, *op. cit.*, p. 61. Fraser's discussion is limited to "diastasis" which he uses to support a view of Mauberley's "passivity" to "prop the comparison of Mauberley to a botanist who has somehow failed to pick out his prize specimen." He pays no attention to the remainder of Mauberley's vocabulary.

5. Paul Elmer More, "Victorian Literature," *Shelburne Essays*, Vol. VII (1910), (Phaeton Press ed., London, 1967), p.268.

6. *Ibid.*, p. 237.

7. For a good introduction to the subject see P. G. Ellis,

"The Development of T. S. Eliot's Historical Sense,"
Review of English Studies, New Series XXIII. 91 (1972),
pp. 291–301.

8. The connections between Pater, Wilde and Pound may
   be seen quite simply by placing together their most
   available statements on "tradition." Pater famously derives the "relative spirit" of the "modern" in his essay on
   Coleridge from the inductive sciences, and in "The
   School of Giorgione" he defines the "moment":

   > ...some brief and wholly concrete moment—into
   > which, however, all the motives, all the interests and
   > effects of a long history, have condensed themselves,
   > and which seem to absorb past and future in an
   > intense consciousness of the present. (*The Renais-
   > sance,* Library edition, London, 1910, p. 150).

   Wilde's Gilbert prescribes the function of "the critical
   spirit" in "The Critic as Artist":

   > ...with the development of the critical spirit we shall
   > be able to realise, not merely our own lives, but the
   > collective life of the race, and so to make ourselves
   > absolutely modern, in the true meaning of the word
   > modernity. For he to whom the present is the only
   > thing that is present, knows nothing of the age in
   > which he lives. To realise the nineteenth century,
   > one must realise every century that has preceded it
   > and that has contributed to its making. (*Complete
   > Works,* ed. Vyvyan Holland, London, 1966, p. 1040).

   Pound assimilates both statements for his "Vortex,"
   translating Wilde's "collective life of the race" into the
   more technical "RACE–MEMORY" the term used by
   More:

   > All experience rushes into this vortex. All the
   > energized past, all the past that is living and worthy
   > to live. ALL MOMENTUM, which is the past bear-
   > ing upon us, RACE, RACE–MEMORY, instinct
   > charging the PLACID, NON–ENERGISED FU-
   > TURE.
   >
   > The DESIGN of the future in the grip of the
   > human vortex. All the past that is vital, all the past

that is capable of living into the future, is pregnant in
the vortex, NOW ("Vortex", *Blast*, I [20 June 1914],
p. 153).

Mauberley ends the poem as "An Hedonist;" on the
same page of "Vortex," Pound defines hedonism as
"the vacant place of a vortex, without force, deprived of
past and future," the "vacant place" of a vortex conceived in the tradition of Pater and Wilde and corre-
sponding to the static centre of metamorphosis in
which the "still stone dogs" are left as epilogues for
Mauberley who is trapped and suspended by both.
Such a suspension is always the danger immanent in
the vortex; Wyndham Lewis notes a few pages earlier:
"the Vorticist is at his maximum point of energy when
stillest," and "Our Vortex desires the *immobile* rhythm of
its swiftness" (my emphasis; p.148).

9. *The Translations of Ezra Pound,* ed. Hugh Kenner, London, 1953, p.18. Pound's debt to Pater here is discussed
by Hugh Witemeyer, *op. cit.,* p.9.

10. On Mauberley's behalf, I think it is often too easy for
readers of Pound to be seduced by the more obvious
aphorisms that he hurled into the battle of literary
London—"The Spirit of the arts is dynamic" etc.; the
vigorous Odyssean image of the poet. It is worth remembering that Pound continually assumes two primary modes of response:

> ...the whole difference between the French and
> Tedescan systems: a German never knows when a
> thought "is only to be thought"—to be thought out in
> all its complexity and its beauty—and when it is to be
> made a basis of action. ("Remy de Gourmont—I,"
> *Pavannes and Divisions,* (New York, 1918), p.115).

11. Of all Wilde's work, "The Critic as Artist" contains most
that Pound would be in sympathy with. It is here that
Wilde celebrates the "unapproachable beauty" of
Gautier's *Symphonie en Blanc Majeur,* that "flawless mas-
terpiece of colour and music" (*Complete Works,* ed. Hol-

land, p.1051), and from his biological stand-point, he can claim "It is Criticism that makes us cosmopolitan" (p.1056). Most significant of all is Wilde's ambition for critical method:

> ...where there is no record, and history is either lost, or was never written, Criticism can re-create the past for us from the very smallest fragment of language or art, just as surely as the man of science can from some tiny bone, or the mere impress of a foot upon a rock, re-create for us the winged dragon or Titan lizard that once made the earth shake beneath its tread, can call Behemoth out of his cave, and make Leviathan swim once more across the startled sea. (p.1056).

The prose is over-inflated, but the principle announced here directs us back to Georges Cuvier, the founder of palaeontology and the only acknowledged master of Louis Agassiz, Pound's own scientific mentor. Cuvier writes in his *Discourse on the Revolutions of the Surface of the Globe:*

> ...a claw, a shoulder-blade, a condyle, a leg or arm bone, or any other bone separately considered, enables us to discover the description of teeth to which they belonged; so also, reciprocally, we may determine the form of the other bones from the teeth. Thus, commencing our investigation by a careful survey of any one bone by itself, a person who is sufficiently master of the laws of organic structure may, as it were, reconstruct the whole animal to which that bone had belonged. (Quoted J. Arthur Thomson, *The Science of Life,* London, 1899, p.29).

For Agassiz, and later for Frobenius, the method offers a practical sanction for the reading of "signatures" in Nature; it holds the same charisma for Pound himself, and above all it sanctifies the "living tradition;" Thomson claims that the task of palaeontology is "to spell out the history of the past, so far as that history can be deciphered from the fossil-bearing rocks, to trace the rise and decline of races, to disclose the sublime spectacle of life's progress." (p.162).

12. "Mr. Villerant's Morning Outburst," *The Little Review,* V. 7 (November 1918), p. 7. Donald Davie was the first to describe Villerant as a model for Mauberley (*The Poet as Sculptor,* pp. 91−101). His excellent account recognizes the ambiguity of Villerant for Pound himself, but it includes no discussion of Villerant's scientific bias.

13. "Mr. Villerant's Morning Outburst," *loc. cit.* p. 11, cf. in particular Pound's demands for a more serious cognitive status for the arts in "The Serious Artist" (1913) and the essays on Joyce, 1917−1918.

14. "W. Villerant to the ex-Mrs. Burn," *The Little Review,* V. 1 (May 1918), p. 53.

15. "Walter Villerant to Mrs. Bland Burn," *The Little Review,* IV. 5 (September 1917), p. 20.

16. For Pound, it is an image that in part is propagated by Ford Madox Ford who continually swiped against "the English aesthetic poets who were prepared to faint at the smell of lily and to swoon at a glance from a pair of handsome eyes" (*The March of Literature* [1938], London, 1947, pp. 343−344).

17. "Walter Villerant to Mrs. Bland Burn," *The Little Review,* IV. 6 (October 1917), p. 16.

18. "W. Villerant to the ex-Mrs. Burn," *The Little Review,* V. 1 (May 1918), p. 55.

19. "Patria Mia," first published in *The New Age* in eleven installments; XI. 19 (5 September 1912)—XII. 2 (14 November 1912). Reprinted as *Patria Mia and The Treatise on Harmony,* London, 1962, pp. 32−33.

20. "Dubliners" and Mr. James Joyce, *The Egoist,* I. 14 (15 July 1914), p. 267. Three years earlier, Pound had announced: "The truly 'donative' artist discovers, or better, he 'discriminates.' We advance by discriminations..." ("I Gather the Limbs of Osiris, IV," *The New Age,* X. 8 [21 December 1911], p. 179).

21. A. R. Orage, "Mr. Pound and Mr. Wyndham Lewis in

Public," *Readers and Writers (1917–1921)*, (London,
1922), pp. 53–54. Orage distinguishes both Pound and
Wyndham Lewis from "this class of aesthetic val-
etudinarians" as "robust persons with excellent diges-
tions." Interestingly, given Mauberley's "Mildness
amid the neo-Nietzschean clatter," and his "graduations" (impoverished selections) which are "out of
place" under such circumstances, Orage's distinction
occurs in the context of a discussion of the "Will to
Power."

22. G. S. Fraser, *op.cit.*, p.61.
23. John J. Espey, *op.cit.*, p.76n.
24. Remy de Gourmont, *The Natural Philosophy of Love*,
    trans. Ezra Pound (1922), (Casanova Society, London,
    1926), p.180.
25. *Ibid.*, pp. 178, 179.
26. Poincaré, *Science and Method* (1909), trans. Francis
    Maitland, London, 1914, pp. 57–66.
27. See in particular Whitehead's *Principles of Natural
    Knowledge* (London, 1919). Bertrand Russell, in his
    preface to the English translation of Poincaré's *Science
    et Methode*, writes of the chaos of the intellectual climate
    that science had created for itself:

    > Another reason which makes a philosophy of sci-
    > ence especially useful at the present time is the revo-
    > lutionary progress, the sweeping away of what had
    > seemed fixed landmarks, which has so far charac-
    > terised this century, especially in physics. The con-
    > ception of the "working hypothesis," provisional,
    > approximate, and merely useful, has more and
    > more pushed aside the comfortable eighteenth cen-
    > tury conception of "laws of nature." *op. cit.* (pp. 6–7)

28. *The Education of Henry Adams* (1905), (Boston & New
    York, 1918), p. 456.
29. Thorstein Veblen, "The Place of Science in Modern
    Civilisation," *The American Journal of Sociology*, XI
    (March 1906). Reprinted in *The Place of Science in Mod-*

ern Civilization and Other Essays (1919), (New York, 1961), pp. 15–16.

30. Karl Pearson, *The Grammar of Science*, (1892), (London, 1900), p. 6 (Introduction to the 2nd Edition). In one of those curious products of what Marshall McLuhan once called the "technological America" of Pound's youth, we find the principle applied to literary criticism: "When we look at the subject from the scientific point of view, the artist disappears" (M. H. Liddell, *An Introduction to the Scientific Study of English Poetry*, Norwood, Mass. and London, 1902, pp. 27– 28). Liddell's point provides a basis for Pound's famous comment that the first sign of bad criticism is the focus on the author rather than on the text.

31. *Ibid.*, p. 87.

32. *Ibid.*, p. 181. cf. A. S. Eddington, "The Meaning of Matter and the Laws of Nature according to the Theory of Relativity," *Mind* N.S, XXIX. 114 (April 1920).

33. Poincaré, *op. cit.*, p. 22.

34. *Ibid.*, p. 23. Pound's admiration for scientific method and for "scientific prose" is well known; it is an admiration for those qualities of hardness, precision, economy and dryness (this last being a lesson mainly from Hulme, but also from the Heraclitean "dry soul" that Pater refers to at the end of *Plato and Platonism*). We are familiar with the major areas in which Pound celebrates such qualities, but there is one area that often goes unnoticed. In a review of 1918 Pound notes of the poetry of Marianne Moore and Mina Loy, "The arid clarity, not without its own beauty, of le tempérament de l'Americaine" ("A List of Books," *The Little Review*, IV.11 [March 1918] p. 57). Mauberley's art exhibits exactly such an "arid clarity"; Pound's use of this quality to describe "le temperament de l'Americaine" serves to remind us of Mauberley's origins.

35. Hudson Maxim, *The Science of Poetry and the Philosophy of*

Language, (New York, 1910), p. ix.

36. *Ibid.*, p. 78.

37. *Ibid.*, p. 85.

38. "The Science of Poetry," *Book News Monthly*, XXIX. 4 (December 1910), pp. 282–283. "The Wisdom of Poetry," *Forum*, New York, XLVII.4 (April 1912), pp. 497–501; reprinted *Selected Prose 1909–1965*, ed. William Cookson, London, 1973.

39. Maxim, *op. cit.*, p. 43. Quoted Pound, "The Wisdom of Poetry," *Selected Prose*, p. 329. Pound had also quoted this definition in his review ("The Science of Poetry," *loc.cit.*, p. 283) where he had admired Maxim's strictures against "dead metaphors."

40. "The Science of Poetry," *loc. cit.*, p. 283.

41. "The Wisdom of Poetry," *Selected Prose*, p. 332. Pound's position here is a distinct advance from a tentative gesture of 1910: "Poetry is a sort of inspired mathematics, which gives us equations, not for abstract figures, triangles, spheres, and the like, but equations for the human emotions." (*The Spirit of Romance*, London, 1910, p. 5).

42. "Reviews," signed "Z", *The New Freewoman*, I.8 (1 October 1913), pp. 149–150.

43. *Ibid.*, p. 150.

44. "Vorticism," *The Fortnightly Review* N.S., XCVI . 573 (1 September 1914), p. 469. Pound's "race-long recurrent moods" is reminiscent of Wilde's "race memory."

45. See A. R. Jones, *The Life and Opinions of T. E. Hulme*, (London, 1960), p. 19.

46. "Notes on Language and Style," published as Appendix III in Michael Roberts, *T. E. Hulme*, (London, 1938), p. 272.

47. *Speculations*, ed. Herbert Read (1924), (London, 1960), p. 224. The connections with the "pyramid" of logic that Fenollosa describes in *The Chinese Written Character as a Medium for Poetry* are self-evident. Bergson similarly sees the method of the exact sciences as purely

conceptual; he writes of the "stationary" quality of concepts in their attempts to "fix" the elements of the "invariable" (*An Introduction to Metaphysics*, trans. T. E. Hulme, [London, 1913], pp. 37–38). Bergson maintains that our customary habit of mind is to seek the "mobility" of the real world in terms of static, immobile concepts, the mind searching for "solid points of support" (p. 56). Obviously enough, such a habit is inevitably at odds with the "durée réele," which Hulme describes thus: "One must think of it as duration, that is to say, continuous growth in creation. A becoming never the same, never repeating itself, but always producing novelty, continually ripening and creating." (*Speculations*, p. 197). It is above all, the "novelty," the unexpected "accidents," produced by evolutionary time that signify the great problem for Mauberley.

48. Pearson, *op. cit.*, p. vii.
49. A. S. Eddington, *The Nature of the Physical World*, (Cambridge, 1928), p. xv.
50. *Ibid.*, p. xiii.
51. *Gaudier-Brzeska. A Memoir* (1916), (Marvell Press edition, London, 1960), p. 91.

Baumann: The Structure of Canto IV

1. Harvey Gross, *Sound and Form in Modern Poetry* (Ann Arbor: The University of Michigan Press, 1964), p. 166.
2. See Gross, pp. 34, 159.
3. Hugh Kenner, *The Pound Era* (London: Faber and Faber, 1972), p. 485.
4. Gross, p. 159.
5. See Walter Baumann, *The Rose in the Steel Dust: An Examination of the Cantos of Ezra Pound* (Coral Gables, Florida: University of Miami Press, 1970), pp. 24–26.
6. Gross, p. 158.
7. "Foreword (1964)" of *A Lume Spento* (London: Faber and Faber, 1965).

8. William E. Baker, *Syntax in English Poetry: 1870–1930* (Berkeley and Los Angeles: University of California Press, 1967), p. 55.

9. *The Spirit of Romance* (London: Peter Owen, 1952), p. 8.

10. *Poems 1918–1921* (New York: Boni and Liveright, 1921).

11. K. L. Goodwin, *The Influence of Ezra Pound* (London: Oxford University Press, 1966), p. 212 and passim.

12. The eighteen Cantos starting with "and" are I, X, XII, XVI, XVIII, XXII, XXVI, XXVIII, XXXVIII, XLIV, XLVI, XLVIII, LII, LVII, LXXVI, LXXVII, XCII, CVI.

13. "As Gyges on Thracian platter set the feast" is the only line in Canto IV where the natural word order is seriously disturbed.

14. " 'Tis. 'Tis. Ytis!" of course becomes "by homonymic metamorphosis *It is*" (Gross, p. 167).

15. See 92/620:653 and 106/752:777.

16. *The Letters of Ezra Pound: 1907–1941*, ed. D. D. Paige (London: Faber and Faber, 1951), p. 386.

17. *Letters*, p. 36.

18. *Collected Shorter Poems* (London: Faber and Faber, 1962), p. 44.

19. *Collected Shorter Poems*, p. 174.

20. Hugh Witemeyer, *The Poetry of Ezra Pound: Forms and Renewal*, 1908–1920 (Berkeley and Los Angeles: University of California Press, 1969), p. 71.

21. Kenner, pp. 417–18.

22. *The Spirit of Romance*, pp. 178, 196.

23. See Kenner, p. 548, and *A Lume Spento*, p. 14.

24. *Collected Shorter Poems*, p. 80.

25. *The Rose in the Steel Dust*, p. 33 and Endnote 72.

26. *Collected Shorter Poems*, p. 17.

27. *Letters*, p. 285.

28. See 2/6:10, 7/24 & 25: 28 & 29 and 20/91:95.

29. Bradford Morrow, "A Source for 'Palace in smoky light': Pound and Dryden's Virgil," *Paideuma* III, 245.

30. Kenner, p. 423.
31. Kenner, p. 93.
32. Kenner, p. 430 (quoting Basil Bunting).
33. See Daniel D. Pearlman, *The Barb of Time: On the Unity of Ezra Pound's Cantos* (New York: Oxford University Press, 1969), p. 56n.
34. *The Rose in the Steel Dust,* pp. 19–53.
35. Eugene Paul Nassar, *The Cantos of Ezra Pound: The Lyric Mode* (Baltimore and London: The Johns Hopkins University Press, 1975), p. 136.

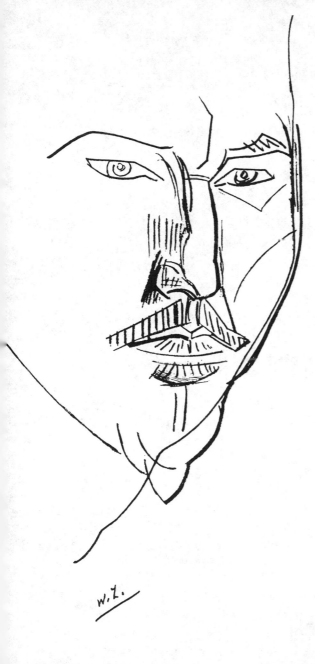

EZRA POUND

The London Years

SHEFFIELD UNIVERSITY LIBRARY

23 April - 13 May 1976

Cover: Pen and ink drawing of Ezra Pound by Wyndham Lewis, 1914
Reproduced by permission of Omar Pound

Previously unpublished material by Ezra Pound, printed by permission of
The Ezra Pound Literary Property Trust and Faber & Faber, Ltd., 1976

All material by Dorothy Pound, copyright Omar Pound, 1976

Introduction and notes, copyright Philip Grover, 1976

FOR OMAR AND ELIZABETH POUND

This Catalogue printed in a
Limited Edition of 450 copies

INTRODUCTION

THE materials gathered together for this exhibition relate, principally, to the period 1908 - 1920. It is an important period in Pound's life and one of immense creative activity. It sees the beginning of his association with Ford Madox Hueffer (Ford) with the publication of "Sestina: Altaforte" in *The English Review* for June 1909 and his long association with Orage's *The New Age* — he wrote over 300 articles for it — which begins in November 1911 with the first of the twelve instalments of "I Gather The Limbs of Osiris". It is the time of his translations from Arnaut Daniel and Guido Cavalcanti, his "Seafarer" and his "Cathay"; it is the time of his various Provençal personæ, of his imitations and recreations of Provençal verse forms, his evocation of Provence in "Provincia Deserta" and his re-construction of Bertrans de Born in "Near Perigord". It is also the period of his lectures at the London Polytechnic, Regent Street, which he published as *The Spirit of Romance* (1910) and attended, amongst others, by Olivia and Dorothy Shakespear, the latter becoming his wife in 1914. It is the time of his association with Gaudier-Brzeska, the creation of Imagisme with Richard Aldington and Hilda Doolittle, of the creation of Vorticism and the friendship with Wyndham Lewis and the publication of the only two numbers of *Blast* in 1914 and 1915. It is the time too of his translations of the Japanese Noh plays from the notes of Ernest Fenollosa and of his campaign to get his "The Chinese Written Character as a Medium of Poetry" published.

Pound came to London in 1908 believing that Yeats was the only living poet worth studying so this is the time too when he was 'learning how Yeats did it', and of their winters together in Stone Cottage, Coleman's Hatch. In 1912 Harriet Monroe started *Poetry* in Chicago and Pound was a contributor from the first number and until February 1919 was the review's "foreign correspondent". It is in these years that Pound first meets T. S. Eliot and James Joyce — the latter through Yeats — and champions and promotes the work of both, often helping also to find funds for them, particularly Joyce. It is the period in which "Homage to Sextus Propertius", "Hugh Selwyn Mauberley" and the first four Cantos — the first three to be substantially altered before becoming those we now know — are first published. This is but a bare outline of the extent of Pound's immense activity, artistic creativity, and enormous promotional zeal. Most of it is represented in this exhibition although as a result of what has been available to us the greatest attention focuses on Pound's connections with Provence, particularly as seen in his translations from Arnaut Daniel and his use of Provençal themes and material in the Fourth Canto. We are indeed most fortunate in having a pictorial and documentary record of the visit Ezra and Dorothy Pound made to France in the spring and summer of 1919.

The Pounds left England via Southampton on 22 April 1919, and arrived in Toulouse on the 24th. EP had been in England since his return from Italy in October 1913 and this was the first opportunity he and Dorothy, who were married in April 1914, had had to go abroad since the start of the war. They were there some four and a half months, not returning to London until September. More than half of this time was spent in the general area of Toulouse which they used as a base. The trip seems to have been partly a pilgrimage to places closely related to the medieval troubadours that Pound already knew well from his trip in 1912 and which he had celebrated in "Provincia Deserta" and "Near Perigord", both of these poems having been published in *Poetry* in 1915 (March and December respectively). But in addition the journey gave an opportunity to Dorothy to paint, the most fruitful inspiration seeming to have been the Pyrenées near Montréjeau and perhaps also those near Mauléon and Foix. They were in Mauléon, Montréjeau and Foix in June and in Montréjeau again for at least several days in July (12-15). Only towards the end of July did they go into the territory of Bertrans de Born, Arnaut Daniel and de Born's Maint, arriving in Brive on 24 July. The Pounds themselves visited Excideuil, Hautefort (or Altaforte), Montignac, Rocamadour, coming back to Brive and arriving once more in Excideuil on 15th August. Dorothy stayed there whilst Ezra and T. S. Eliot — who had joined them at Excideuil, presumably around the 15th of August — went on to Thiviers and Brantôme. However by 23rd August they were all at Brive once more. On 26th August they were at Orléans planning to leave the next day for Paris, where they appear to have spent about two weeks before returning to London on 11th September, three days before Dorothy's birthday.

I give below the chronology of the Pounds' trip in 1919 in so far as I have been able to establish it from consulting the postcards they sent back to Mr. and Mrs. Shakespear or those Ezra sent to Dorothy when he was walking with Eliot and she was staying behind in Excideuil. This slightly corrects (as well as supplementing) the account given by Noel Stock in his *The Life of Ezra Pound* (London, 1970, pp. 224-225). I have as a result some doubts as to whether T. S. Eliot could have been with them when they were in the region of Montségur as Hugh Kenner claims. (*The Pound Era*, pp. 333-335) He is right in saying that Eliot joined them at Excideuil but as previously noted they were not there before 25th July and none of their cards after that date are sent from any place further south than Brive. All of their southern visits seem to have been made from 24th April to 24th July, before their first arrival in Excideuil.

I also have some reservations about Kenner's claim that Pound was at Saint-Bertrand-de-Comminges on 12th July (p. 338). The only time that Saint-Bertrand is mentioned on any card is on one sent on 6th June from Montréjeau; the Pounds were at Mauléon around the 15th of June and at Montréjeau again from the 12th to the 15th of July. Since Saint-Bertrand lies between Mauléon and Montréjeau they *could* have been at Saint-Bertrand any one of these times — it is merely not certain, from the evidence, that EP was actually there on 12th July itself.

This trip marks the beginning of the end of Pound's residence in England. For on 26th April 1920 he and Dorothy left England again, this time for Italy. They were in Paris in June and July, and although they returned to London towards the end of July they did not remain there long, Pound deciding that 'The Island of Paris' was the one spot in Europe in which to live. By the end of the year therefore he and Dorothy were established at 70bis Notre Dame des Champs. Hence, although we are showing editions of *The Cantos* printed in Paris or London later than 1920 it is fitting that all the works for which we have manuscripts and that everything shown here except for two Cantos — and these are closely associated with themes and experiences of this time — were all completed during the London years.

CHRONOLOGY OF THE POUNDS' TRIP TO FRANCE IN 1919
(as established from their postcards, identity cards and passports)

April	22	Departure from England via Southampton
	24	Arrival in Toulouse
June	6	Montréjeau (Haute-Garonne)
	7	Toulouse
	11	Toulouse
	circa 15	Mauléon (Haute-Garonne)
	22	Foix
	28	Foix (Peace just signed)
July	12-15	Montréjeau
	24	Brive (Corrèze)
	25	Excideuil
	28	Clermont-Ferrand
August	1	Hautefort
	2	Montignac
	5	Rocamadour and Brive
	15	Excideuil (Dorothy Pound stays here while Ezra and T. S. Eliot journey on foot)
	17	Thiviers (TSE and EP)
	18	Brantôme (TSE and EP)
	23	Brive
	26	Orléans
September	11	Return to 5 Holland Place Chambers, London

NOTE: They also visited Montségur, Roquefixade, Lavelanet, Carcassonne, Beaucaire, St. Gilles, Arles (Stock mentions Nîmes and Avignon as well), Mareuil, and perhaps Albi, Allègre and Le Puy en Vélay but it is not possible to give the exact dates of these from the evidence I have so far seen.

CHRONOLOGY OF THE WORKS SHOWN IN THIS EXHIBITION

1909   *Exultations*
           The Poems of Ernest Dowson

1910   *The Spirit of Romance*

1911   *Post Liminium: Essays and Critical Papers* by Lionel Johnson

1912   *Sonnets and Ballate of Guido Cavalcanti*

1915   *Cathay*
           Poetical Works of Lionel Johnson with *Preface* by Ezra Pound

1916   *Lustra* — English edition
           Blast 2

1917   *Lustra* — American edition

1919   *The Fourth Canto*
           Quia Pauper Amavi

1920   *Instigations*
           Hugh Selwyn Mauberley
           Umbra

1925   *A Draft of XVI Cantos*

1928   *A Draft of Cantos 17-27*

1937   *The Fifth Decad of Cantos*

Works cited in the following notes.

Cookson — *Selected Prose 1909-1965*, by Ezra Pound, edited with an Introduction by William Cookson, London, 1973.

Edwards and Vaase — *Annotated Index to the Cantos of Ezra Pound, Cantos I — LXXXIV*, by John Hamilton Edwards and William W. Vaase, University of California, 1971.

Gallup — *A Bibliography of Ezra Pound*, by Donald Gallup, London, 1973.

Ruthven — *A Guide to Ezra Pound's "Personae" (1926)*, by K. K. Ruthven, University of California, 1969.

EZRA POUND

the London Years

(1)   A DRAFT OF | XVI | CANTOS OF EZRA POUND | for the Beginning of a Poem | of some Length | now first made Into a Book | with Initials by | HENRY SLATER | (*device*) | PARIS | THREE MOUNTAINS PRESS | MCMXXV.

Number 56 of the copies printed on Roma paper. Title page bears Dorothy Pound's signature.

(2)   Manuscript draft of part of Canto IV.

By comparing the manuscript with the printed version one can notice the changes, usually in the form of further condensation and economy of phrase, that EP made before reaching his final version. Study of the manuscript also seems to suggest that he thought and composed in short phrases — these are usually marked off at the end of or between lines by a double dash. These short phrases thus separated in the manuscript are sometimes linked together to form a longer line in the final version.

(3)   Further pages of the manuscript draft. These deal with Vidal, Actæon, the nymphs bathing in water, and the church roof in Poitiers. All the manuscript material we have hence relates to Provence.

(4)   THE FOURTH CANTO | by | EZRA POUND | Forty | Copies of this poem, numbered 1-40 | on Japanese Vellum set up and privately printed | by John Rodker. Completed | 4th October 1919 | This is No. 5 | (*Device*) | THE OVID PRESS.

The device and initial letter are from designs by Edward Wadsworth.

This is the second state. Line 9 (p. 3): 'Ivory dipping in silver' was added at this printing (See Gallup, p. 48). Study of the manuscript shows that EP had already intended this, the omission obviously being a printer's error. There are some differences between this edition and that published by the Three Mountains Press in 1925 (No. 1) thus p. 3 line 17 up, instead of 'whirls up the bright brown sand' the 1925 and later editions read, 'beneath the knees of the gods.' The line 'The water whirls up the bright pale sand in the spring's mouth' is then added between lines 13 and 14 up in the later editions, and the parentheses and inverted commas are removed from '("The pines at Takasago grow with the pines of Ise")'. Line 12 up becomes 'forked-branch tips' rather than 'The forked tips'. In line 6 up EP has added in later editions '(as at Gourdon that time)'. Line 5 up: 'The saffron sandal petals the tender foot, Hymenæus' becomes 'Saffron sandal so petals the narrow foot: Hymenæus Io!' and line 2 up, 'Amaracus, Hill of Urania's Son' is omitted. The last line, 'Meanwhile So Gioku' is altered to 'And So Gioku, saying' in 1925, the present editions omitting the 'And'.

There are a number of changes on the last page and the simplest procedure would seem to be to give the text of 1919 from 'Grey stone-posts leading nowither' to the end of the passage and let the reader compare this with the current text of Canto IV given at the end of this catalogue.

Gray stone-posts leading nowither.
The Spanish poppies swim in an air of glass.
Père Henri Jacques still seeks the sennin on Rokku.
Polhonac,
As Gyges on Thracian platter, set the feast;

Cabestan, Terreus.
     It is Cabestan's heart in the dish.
Vidal, tracked out with dogs . . . for glamour of Loba;
Upon the gilded tower in Ecbatan
     Lay the god's bride, lay ever
Waiting the golden rain.
     Et saave!
But today, Garonne is thick like paint, beyond Dorada,
The worm of the Procession bores in the soup of the
                              crowd,
The blue thin voices against the crash of the crowd
     At "Salve REGina".
In trellises
     Wound over with small flowers, beyond Adige
In the but half -used room, thin film of images,
     (by Stefano)
Age of unbodied gods, the vitreous fragile images
Thin as the locust's wing
Haunting the mind . . . as of Guido . . .
Thin as the locust's wing. The Centaur's heel
Plants in the earth-loam.

(5)   Two postcards from Dorothy and Ezra Pound's trip to France in 1919.

    (a) The church Notre-Dame-la-Grande

The lines:

'Like a fish-scale roof
    Like the church roof in Poitiers
If it were gold.'; were inspired by the roof of Notre-Dame-la-Grande. However even in the strongest sun the roof, which is of a dull grey stone, can hardly be said to glitter. The image is not provided by nature except for the scale-like shapes on the roof; the colour, the gold, and hence the glittering is an act of his creative visual imagination.

    (b) La Cathédrale Saint-Pierre, Poitiers.

(6)   Saint-Hilaire, Poitiers.

    Architecturally Poitiers was of considerable interest to EP. 'St-Hilaire its proportion' (Canto LI, but also see Canto XLV) is in Poitiers and becomes one of his examples of the cleanness of line before the decadence of the arts caused by Usura. The superiority of Romanesque over Gothic or Renaissance architecture goes back, however, to the period of *The Spirit of Romance*. When in Saint-Hilaire in 1974 I was told by the verger that an American — presumably an architectural student from what he said — had been there some time before making detailed measurements and telling him that it was perfectly proportioned! Have EP's ideas begun to influence the study of the history of Architecture in America?

(7)   Postcard: La Haute-Garonne. Montréjeau—vue sur la Vallée de la Garonne et Polignan.

    The card is addressed to Mrs. Shakespear (Dorothy Pound's mother, Olivia Shakespear who was a minor novelist in her own right and friend of W. B. Yeats. In his *Memoirs* she appears under the pseudonym of "Diana Vernon."). It is dated 12th July 1919. The message reads, in part, "View from balcony. Coz industriously painting." ('Coz' is Dorothy Pound).

    The Pounds left England on 22nd April 1919; a card sent by EP on 24th April to Mrs. Shakespear announced their arrival in Toulouse. On the back of a postcard of the Basilique Saint-Sernin, Toulouse, collected at the time of this trip, Dorothy Pound noted in 1970 that 'We got permits to leave England & go here — "Papa Dulac" found us a room & gave us many meals . . . We stayed many weeks & took walks from this as centre.'

In *Canto LXXX* first published in 1946 EP evokes this aspect of their journey:

> But Tosch the great ex-greyhound
> used to get wildly excited
> at being given large beefsteaks
> in Tolosa
> and leapt one day finally
> right into the centre of the large dining table
> and lay there as a centre piece
> near the cupboard piled half full
> with novels of 'Willy', etc.,
> in the old one franc editions
> and you cd | hear papa Dulac's voice
> clear in the choir that wd | ring ping on the high altar
> in the Bach chorals
> true as a pistol shot

(8) Postcard: La Haute-Garonne. Montréjeau. Le Clocher.

On Sunday 6th June 1919 Dorothy Pound sent this card to her mother at 12 Brunswick Gardens, London. 'A large packet arrived safely, with Q and papers to sign. We have a room with a view of dozen of Pyrenées — Its been very cloudy — But we have had two (small!) walks. The cooking is more like Italian with saffron & cinammon, etc., in it. We saw our beloved St. Bertrand in the distance round a hill. I daresay we shall slink back for a day or so! Love D.' (Q. here refers to *Quia Pauper Amavi*. See No. 54).

(9) EZRA POUND | THE FIFTH DECAD OF | CANTOS | (ideograms) | FABER & FABER | LONDON

E
—
First edition, 1937. Copy inscribed by EP: 'D. her copy Æ '

The lower of these characters is one of Pound's key terms: chêng⁴ meaning variously 'correct, straight, regular; to govern; the first, principal; just, precisely.' Used by Pound in the sense of 'clear as to definitions.' (Canto 67)

(10) Postcard: Saint-Bertrand-de-Comminge (Haute-Garonne)

| | From Val Cabrere, were two miles of roofs to San Bertrand |

Canto XLVIII:
> From Val Cabrere, were two miles of roofs to San Bertrand
> so that a cat need not set foot in the road
> where now is an inn, and bare rafters,
> where they scratch six feet deep to reach pavement
> where now is wheat field, and a milestone
> an altar to Terminus, with arms crossed
> back of the stone
> Where sun cuts light against evening;
> where light shaves grass into emerald
> Savairic; hither Gaubertz;

(11) Two small and one larger water-colour sketches of the Pyrenées by Dorothy Pound, 1919. They are probably from Montréjeau although they may possibly be from Mauléon (both of which are only a few kilometres from Saint-Bertrand). In a card sent from Foix on 22nd June 1919 to Mrs. Shakespear EP wrote: 'Subj. for family artist awaiting treatment from this window. 3d Tower would go onto canvas with rushing water, etc. . . .' and he provided a rough sketch of the castle of Foix. No water colour of this castle on its rock by Dorothy Pound has come to light.

(12) Three water colours of the Pyrenées by Dorothy Pound.

(a) 13″ × 8″   approximately
(b) 9½″ × 10¾″ approximately
(c) 6″ × 11″   approximately

These are all signed and dated 'D. Shakespear 1919'.

(13) Six water colour sketches of the Pyrenées by D. Shakespear all dated 1919.

(a) $3\frac{1}{2}'' \times 9\frac{1}{4}''$ (d) $4'' \times 9\frac{1}{4}''$
(b) $2\frac{3}{4}'' \times 9\frac{1}{4}''$ (e) $4\frac{1}{4}'' \times 9\frac{1}{4}''$
(c) $4'' \times 9\frac{1}{4}''$ (f) $4'' \times 9\frac{1}{4}''$

(14) POST LIMINIUM: ESSAYS | AND CRITICAL PAPERS | By LIONEL JOHNSON | Edited by Thomas White More | (*device*) | ELKIN MATHEWS VIGO STREET | LONDON MCMXI.

The fly leaf bears the inscription 'O.S. Xmas 1911 from D.S.' Pound's own copy bears the inscription 'Ezra Pound 10 Church Walk, W.'

(15) POETICAL WORKS OF | LIONEL JOHNSON | (*Device*) | LONDON: ELKIN MATHEWS | CORK STREET MCMXV.

The frontispiece is a photograph of Lionel Johnson taken at Winchester School in 1885. This copy is inscribed: 'Ezra Pound. With Publisher's regards. Oct. 26, 1915.'

This volume contains a preface by Ezra Pound which was not included in the American edition issued by Macmillan of New York in December 1915. That edition was made up of the English sheets bound in America. The later English editions published by Elkin Mathews in 1917 and 1926 also do not contain the preface which can most easily now be found in *Literary Essays*, 361-70.

The preface contains the following passage which shows clearly why Pound felt Johnson to be worthy of his attention. 'Their (the poems') appeal is not so much to the fluffy, unsorted imagination of adolescence as to more hardened passion and intellect of early middle-age. I cannot speak more than that. They hold their own now, not perhaps as a whole, but because of certain passages, because of that effect of neatness and hardness.

'In the midst of enthusiasms one thinks perhaps that, if Gautier had not written, Johnson's work might even take its place in Weltliteratur, that it might stand for this clearness and neatness. In English literature it has some such place.' (pp. xiv-xv).

In this same preface (p. xv) Pound explains the significance of *Post Liminium* and further places Johnson. 'The "Post Liminium" is a complete world of culture; his own, wrought out of worthy things . . . He really knew the tradition, the narrow tradition, that is, of English, Latin, and Greek. This intelligent acquaintance with the past differentiates him from the traditionalists of his time, and ours.' There are also other reasons for Pound's seeing in Johnson a worthy predecessor: Johnson's serious interest in technique, 'certainly a distinction among "the poets of England" '. He would have welcomed, says Pound, *vers libre* for he would have known how the Greeks used it. And 'his hatred of slovenliness would have equalled your own.'

(16) Obituary notice of the death of Lionel Johnson, who died 4th October 1902 Lionel Johnson was a relation of Dorothy Pound's, first cousin to Olivia Shakespear.

(17) THE POEMS OF | ERNEST DOWSON | with a Memoir by | ARTHUR SYMONDS | FOUR ILLUSTRATIONS BY | AUBREY BEARDSLEY | with a Portrait by | WILLIAM ROTHENSTEIN | LONDON: JOHN LANE, THE BODLEY HEAD | NEW YORK: JOHN LANE COMPANY MCMIX.

The rear fly-leaf has Victor Plarr's poem "Epitaphium Citharistriae" from the *Book of the Rymer's Club* copied out in Pound's own hand. In an article in *Poetry* for January 1913, commenting on the literary state of things in London, Pound wrote: 'His volume, *In The Dorian Mood*, has been half forgotten, but not his verses Epitaphium Citharistriae.' This praise is somewhat qualified by the subsequent remark that 'it is one thing to take pleasure in a man's work and another to respect him as a great artist'. However EP often visited him in his early years in London and in the April 1915 issue of *Poetry* he reviewed Plarr's *Ernest Dowson*. He appears under the pseudonym of M. Verog in "Hugh Selwyn Mauberley".

(18) Hugh Selwyn | Mauberley | by | EP | (*device*) | THE OVID PRESS | 1920 (The title is in black, the device in blue).

Colophon (p. 29): This edition of 200 copies is the Third Book of the Ovid Press: was printed by John Rodker: and completed 23rd April 1920. OF THIS EDITION: 15 Copies on Japanese Vellum numbered 1-15 and not for sale. 20 Signed copies 16-35, 165 Unsigned copies numbered 36-200 the initials and Colophon by E. Wadsworth.

This particular copy is "out of series" and bears no number; bound in brown boards and green cloth back. It was Dorothy Pound's copy and bears her initials.

In "Siena Mi Fe', Disfecemi Maremma" (p. 15) Pound refers to Victor Plarr, Lionel Johnson and Ernest Dowson.

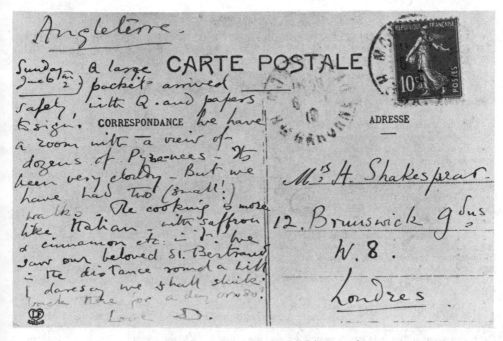

Exhibit No. 8 from the Exhibition catalogue.

(19)   Postcard of Portail de la Dalbade, Toulouse.

This was sent to Mrs. Shakespear on 29th May 1919. EP asked his mother-in-law to "Please send the "Razo" (an nothing else) of the Arnaut Daniel to T. S. Eliot 18 Crawford Mansions Crawford St. W.1" The "Razo" is Pound's imitation of this Provençal form of critical commentary. It only has the appearance of a translation achieved by his use of certain archaic forms of expression. Into this account he has incorporated a number of important critical judgments about Arnaut Daniel.

This "Razo" appeared in *Instigations* published by Boni & Liveright, New York, 1920 and in *Art & Letters* N.S.III.2 (Spring 1920). It was reprinted in *Make It New* (1934) and *Literary Essays* (1954). Pound approached Cecil Palmer about the possibility of an English edition. Palmer replied on 3rd December 1920 that he did not feel able to take it on at the moment although he did agree to act as the distributor for "The Dial".

Arnaut Daniel was probably the most important of all the troubadour poets for Pound. He devoted a whole chapter in *The Spirit of Romance*, this "Razo" with its translations in *Instigations* and a large part of "I Gather the Limbs of Osiris" (which appeared in *The New Age* from 30th November 1911 to 22nd February 1912) to him. In those articles he tells us that 'the "donative" author seems to draw down into the art something which was not in the art of his predecessors . . . He discovers, or better, "he discriminates" . . . We advance by discriminations, and to Arnaut Daniel we may ascribe discriminations.' Furthermore 'Intense hunger for a strict accord between these three (words, rhythm, and music) has marked only the best lyric periods, and Arnaut felt this hunger more keenly and more precisely than his fellows or forerunners' (Cookson, 25-27). And more than once does he praise his 'precision of observation and reference . . . in the language beyond metaphor, by the use of the picturesque verb with an exact meaning.'

(20) INSTIGATIONS | OF | EZRA POUND | TOGETHER WITH | AN ESSAY | ON THE | CHINESE | WRITTEN | CHARACTER | BY | ERNEST FENOLLOSA | BONI AND LIVERIGHT | PUBLISHERS NEW YORK.

The book bears this dedication: To My Father Homer L. Pound.

Inscribed 'To be returned to O. Shakespear, ~~12~~ ~~Brunswick~~ ~~Gardens~~ 34 Abingdon Cou Kensington W.' and later, 'AB' (Agnes Bedford).

(21) Rough draft of a translation of the second and third stanzas of Arnaut Daniel's 'Autet e bas entrels prims fuoills'.

This translation was first published in 'I Gather the Limbs of Osiris, VII. Arnaut Daniel: Canzoni of His Middle Period', *New Age* X. ii (11th January 1912) 249-51 and then incorporated, on pp. 302-4, into the essay which appeared in *Instigations*. It was also republished in *Umbra* (1920) 114-115 and in *The Translations* (1953), 156-159. The whole article was republished in *Make It New* (1934) 43-92 and *Literary Essays* (1954) 109-148.

In *The Spirit of Romance* (1910, p. 29) Pound had already drawn the attention of his readers to the 'imitation of the bird note' which occurs in 'Cadahus | En son us' and recurs in the following five stanzas. In *Instigations* he comes back to this, remarking that ' "Autet e bas" is interesting for the way in which Arnaut breaks the flow of the poem to imitate the bird call . . . and the repetitions of this sound in the succeeding strophes, highly treble, presumably.' Pound renders this with the rhymes 'loose, spruce, reduce, noose', etc.

According to Omar Pound this was one of his favourite poems, if not the favourite poem, from Arnaut Daniel. He knew it by heart and was constantly recommending it to others for its rhythm and rhyme. He urged Omar to learn it too. I leave it to others to pursue the place of bird song in the Cantos as a whole but it is worth remarking that in Canto LXXV the transcription of the Jannequin madrigal is preceded by the line 'not of one bird but many' and that this madrigal itself is one in which Pound found an essential imitation of bird song.

Comparison of the manuscript with the published translation will show the changes EP made in the course of composition.

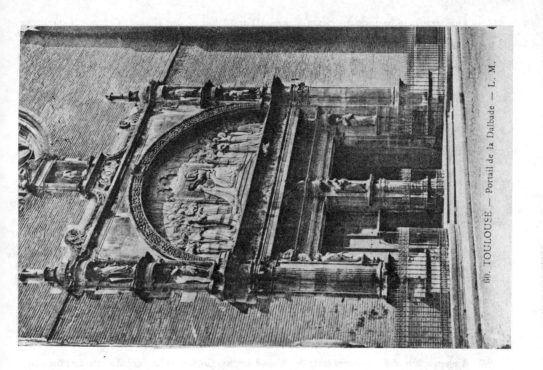

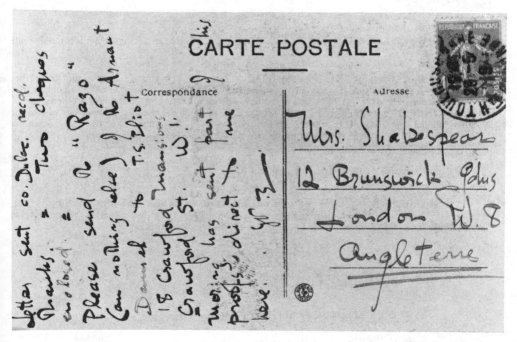

Exhibit No. 19 from the Exhibition catalogue.

(22) This appears to be a rough draft of Stanzas III and IV of Arnaut Daniel's Canzone 'Lanquan vei fueill'e flor e frug', the first stanza of which was published in *Instigations* in 1920 (reprinted in *Make It New*, *The Translations* and *Literary Essays*. Gallup incorrectly ascribes a reprinting in *Umbra*). The Provençal text that Pound used came from *La Vita e le Opere del Trovatore Arnaldo Daniello* edited by U. A. Canello, Halle, 1883, pp. 100-101. The Provençal text shown here is, however, that of the recent critical edition of the *Canzoni* by Gianluigi Toja (Florence, 1960), pp. 221-223.

Pound seems to have abandoned the attempt at a complete translation of this poem as only his version of the first stanza was ever published. The manuscript is interesting not only for the way it shows how he interpreted as well as translated the original, but also for the series of rhymes he tried out to match the original's repeated rhyme scheme. Daniel used a scheme of ababcde throughout the six stanzas, the coda rhyming cdd, and Pound, in his first stanza, succeeded in achieving the same scheme. Although the first four lines of the second stanza repeat the rhyme scheme of a b a b he seems also to have experimented with 'employ, annoy' or 'employing, cloying', a rhyme not used in the first stanza at all. To have used the new scheme would have entailed therefore the rewriting of the first stanza. Does this perhaps explain why he abandoned the translation?

(23) LUSTRA | OF | EZRA POUND | 200 copies privately printed, of which this is No. 1.

Published in 1916.

The circular stamp in orange-red was designed by Edmund Dulac and bears Ezra Pound's initials in intaglio. When Pound came to study Chinese he found that the ideogram Yin⁴ meaning 'a seal, to seal, print' and which is formed from the two characters meaning 'a hand holding a piece of jade, the seal of office, and using it downwards', made the same shapes. He was, I have been told, greatly pleased by the coincidence.

This copy was Dorothy Pound's and bears the Pound's address at this time: 5 Holland Place Chambers, Kensington, W. It is one of the original 200 unexpurgated copies.

(24) A photograph of Ezra Pound taken by Alvin Langdon Coburn. This served as the frontispiece to *Lustra*.

(25) Another copy of *Lustra*. This belonged to Olivia Shakespear and bears her signature. It is number 58.

(26) Miniature of Pound by Mrs. Brunton, 1913, when he was living in Kensington and before his marriage to Dorothy Shakespear which took place in April, 1914. The painting is 3½" in diameter, the overall dimensions being 6⅛" × 6⅛". This is the only known miniature of Pound and pre-dates any of the known drawings or paintings of him by Wyndham Lewis, but not the well-known bust of him by Gaudier-Brzeska. One can note that his hair is not red, and in his description of himself entered on his Identity Card in 1916 he gives the colour of his hair and beard as 'yellowish-brown'.

(27) Typescript draft of Section II of "The Social Order", first published in *Blast 2* (July, 1915) and then in *Lustra*.

This typescript was sent to Mrs. Shakespear (the envelope is addressed in Pound's own hand) *circa* 1914/15. By comparison with the printed text in *Lustra* (item 25) one can notice that EP made some slight changes after this draft was sent.

"FOR AN OLD BITCH GONE IN THE TEETH"

(28) Postcard: Toulouse — Vue générale sur le Marché des Carmes.

This card was sent to Mrs. Shakespear by Ezra Pound on 11th June 1919. On it he wrote: 'Have told dryad she can return to H.P.C. *Anyone* who is going to buy Gaudier portfolio shd be told to do so *at once*. Press cant go on unless initial sales warrant it.' 'Dryad' was H.D., Hilda Doolittle; H.P.C. stands for Holland Place Chambers, the Pounds' flat in London. The portfolio of twenty of Gaudier-Brzeska's drawings was printed by John Rodker for the Ovid Press.

(29) LUSTRA | of EZRA POUND | with Earlier Poems | For Private Circulation | Sixty Copies Printed. New York, October 1917. | This is Number 7.

This copy bears EP's initials on the title page and the initials 'D.P.' (in ink) and the inscription 'D. Pound, 5 Holland Place Chambers, London W.8' (in pencil) in Ezra Pound's handwriting on the fly-leaf.

The frontispiece is a reproduction of a drawing of Pound by Gaudier-Brzeska.

This edition was distributed gratis, mainly by John Quinn and contains a number of poems not found in the English editions (for details see Gallup p. 42). For example, at the end of the volume are published "Three Cantos"; this was their first book publication and preceded that in *Quia Pauper Amavi* by some two years. There are a number of pencilled corrections in EP's handwriting in this volume but only those affecting Canto II ever seem to have been published, finding their way into the text printed in *Quia* (all three differ radically from what are now Cantos I-III).

This volume is in a damaged state because it was buried by Dorothy Pound in a rubbish heap during the Second World War to prevent the Germans from finding it. (see No. 32)

(30) Poem V, Part I of "Hugh Selwyn Mauberley". This is another copy of the first edition, Number 57, and bears the bookplate of John Berryman. Lent by Mr. John Haffenden.

(31) *BLAST 2* for July 1915 with Gaudier-Brzeska's article.

The obituary of Gaudier-Brzeska which appeared in "The Pall Mall Gazette" is simply a reprint of this article and the very wording of the notice of his death is almost the same as that printed in *Blast*. The article was reprinted again in Pound's memoir of Gaudier-Brzeska published in 1916 and can be easily found in the current re-print of that book.

(32) (*In black*) A DRAFT OF | THE CANTOS 17-27 OF EZRA POUND: (*in red*) Initials | by Gladys Hynes | (*in black*) JOHN RODKER — LONDON 1928.

The fly-leaf bears the following inscription: 'This copy was buried in the rubbish-heap of Signora Andaea's garden, for safety — Rapallo during World War II, retrieved in '46 by D.P. given to Omar ap '62. Dorothy Pound Sept. '69'.

(33)   Came home, home to a lie
                                             home to many deceits
                                             home to old lies and new infamy.

This is another copy of No. 32, one of the four copies printed on Vellum and signed by Gladys Hynes and Ezra Pound. It is copy A.

"PROVINCIA DESERTA"

(34) I have climbed rickety stairs, heard talk of Croy.

Postcard: Les vieux Châteaux de Dordogne — Château de Paluel (XIIme Siècle) Situé dans la commune de Saint-Vincent, près Sarlat. Au Moyen-Age, les comtes de Vigier y séjournèrent pendant plus de 300 ans. Complètement démantelé pendant la Guerre de Cent Ans, la famille de Gimel le reconstruisit vers la fin du XVme siècle. Actuellement ce château appartient au prince de Croy.

The de Croy family was a powerful noble family in the Artois, Hainaut and Picardy regions of North-east France, and issued from Kings of Hungary. I have been unable to discover any connection between them and the troubadours or Provence before their ownership of this castle, presumably at the end of the nineteenth or beginning of the twentieth century.

(35)   Have seen Narbonne, and Cahors and Chalus . . .
        'Here Coeur-de-lion was slain . . . '

Postcard: Chalus — Vue du Rocher historique où fut blessé Richard Cœur de Lion en 1198. There is no message from either DP or EP on this card. According to A. L. Poole (*From Domesday Book to Magna Carta*) it was whilst besieging the castle of Chalus to punish a baron of the Limousin in a trivial dispute over treasure trove that Richard I was struck in the shoulder by an arrow. He died from his wound on 6th April 1199.

Pound would have been interested in Richard because of his many connections and associations with the troubadours. He himself composed poetry in both *langue d'oc* and *langue d'oil*; the troubadour Giraut de Bornelh is reputed to have been on the third crusade with him; "if . . . Arnaut frequented one court more than another it was the court of King Richard Coeur de Lion, 'Plantagenet', in compliment to whose sister (presumably) he rimes to 'genebres' in Canzon XVI" (*I Gather the Limbs of Osiris*, IV); he was involved in the complicated power struggles in Aquitaine and France in which Bertrans de Born was more than once implicated; and his death was celebrated in a moving *planh* by Gaucelm Faidit. This last was adapted by Pound in *Five Troubadour Songs* published in 1920, Agnes Bedford helping him with the music.

(36)   I have walked
                    into Perigord,
            I have seen the torch-flames, high-leaping,
            Painting the front of that church;
            Heard, under the dark, whirling laughter.
            I have looked back over the stream
                    and seen the high building,
            Seen the long minarets, the white shafts.

Postcard: Perigueux — La Cathédrale Saint-Front.

Dorothy Pound in a note written on the back of this card in 1970 asks: 'Did I see this ? EP anyway knew it.'

(37) Have seen Excideuil, carefully fashioned.

Postcard: Excideuil (Dordogne) Porte d'entrée du Château de Talleyrand Perigord.

Dorothy wrote to her father, Henry Hope Shakespear on 25th July 1919: 'Please forward letters to us at Hotel Poujol Excideuil Dordogne "until further orders". It is a small village with lovely ruins — of towers, & a Chateau, & this entrance gate. I will write in a day or so.'

On the back of another postcard of the ancient castle Dorothy Pound recorded, many years later — probably in 1969 or 1970 — that they had spent 'several days here — TSE joined us.'

And on another card sent to her father on 15th August 1919 she wrote: 'Please do not forward any more letters to us here, as we think of moving Northwards. It is very hot. Have helped to paint a "cot" for the Patmore's grandchild! Otherwise it is too hot to move much. Our room is well decorated with flypapers — & we introduced one into the kitchen.'

Dorothy seems to have stayed here whilst EP and Eliot went on to Brantôme and Thiviers (see 38-41).

The troubadour Guiraut de Bornelh was born in the region of Excideuil in a noble castle belonging to the Viscount of Limoges. He himself was of humble parentage, however. The dates of his life are uncertain; some give his birth as 1138, others as late as 1165. He is given credit for writing the first *canso*. From EP's comments in *The Spirit of Romance* it would appear that he was not one of the troubadours who meant very much to him.

The first Talleyrand was Guillaume, the husband of Bertrans de Born's Maent. They were a branch of the ancient Counts of Périgord. Pound gives the name as 'Tairiran' in 'Near Perigord' but the usual spelling seems to have been 'Talairan'.

(38) Postcard: Brantôme — La Porte des Réformés où eut lieu l'entrevue de Brantôme et de Coligny, en juin 1569.

(39) Xerox copy of the verso of (38). The card is addressed to Mrs. Pound at Hotel Poujol, Excideuil, and dated 18-8 (1919).

'Brantôme reached & pleasing. T. has 7 blisters. Will probably proceed by train tomorrow. Sunday 5.30 p.m.' (T. is of course T. S. Eliot.)

(40) Postcard: Château de Thiviers (Dordogne)
This card is dated 17.8 (1919) and addressed to Mrs. Pound at Hotel Poujol, Excideuil, Dordogne.

(41) The verso of (40) reads: 'Thiviers reached without incident. Mist this a.m. Chateau Fezloli no postcard available. Love E. Sunday a.m.'

(42)
> I have lain in Roquefixada,
> level with sunset,
> Have seen the copper come down
> tingeing the mountains,
> I have seen the fields, pale, clean as an emerald.

Postcard: L'Ariège. Roquefixade. Le Rocher du Château.

Dorothy Pound's note of 1970 states: 'E.P. & D.P. Sheltered against a wall — rain-storm. 11 a.m. We had started very early — 7 or so a.m. from (word undecipherable) & ended up at Foix.'

(43) Postcard: Roquefixade — Ruines du Château (Côté Nord).

(44)
> Mareuil to the north-east,
> La Tour,
> There are three keeps near Mareuil
> And an old woman
> glad to hear Arnaut,
> Glad to lend one dry clothing.

Postcard: Château de Mareuil (Dordogne).

The card informs us that Mareuil was one of the four first baronies of the Province and that it too passed into the hands of the Talleyrand-Perigords. It was also the birthplace of the poet Arnaut de Marueuill a clerk of poor origin. In *The Spirit of Romance* Pound gives a translation of three of the four stanzas of his Canso 'Belh m'es quan lo vens m'alena' and says of him that 'For the simplicity of adequate speech Arnaut of Marvoil is to be numbered among the best of the courtly "makers"'. Pound also celebrated him in his very Browningesque poem 'Marvoil'.

"I HAVE THOUGHT OF THEM LIVING"

(45)
> Chalais is high, a-level with the poplars . . .
> At Chalais
> is a pleached arbour;
> Old pensioners and old protected women
> Have the right there —
> it is charity.

Postcard: Chalais — Château de "Talleyrand-Perigord" (Tour du XIVe siecle).

On the back of this card Dorothy Pound has recorded her impression of the local pronunciation: 'Dalleyrand Berrigord'.

Pound, in his note to 'Na Audiart', tells us that Bertrans de Born, to make his 'dompna soiseubuda', a borrowed lady, took 'of the Vicomtess of Chalais her throat and two hands.'

(46)
> I have seen Foix on its rock . . .
> Foix between its streams

Postcard: Foix (Ariège) La Préfecture et les Tours.

On the back of another postcard Dorothy Pound recorded: 'EP & DP. We walked into Foix, flags flying. *Peace* just signed. 1919.' (See also 11).

(47)
> So I take my road
> To Rochechouart,
> Swift-foot to my Lady Anhes,
> Seeing that Tristan's lady Iseutz had never
> Such grace of locks . . .

Postcard: Rochecouart (Hte-Vienne) — La Château — Les Arcades.

(48)
>At Rochecoart,
>Where the hills part
>>in three ways,
>And three valleys, full of winding roads,
>Fork out to south and north,
>There is a place of trees . . . gray with lichen.
>I have walked there
>>thinking of old days.

Postcard: Rochecouart (Hte-Vienne) — Vue générale.

(49)
>And from Mauleon, fresh with a new earned grade,
>In maze of approaching rain-steps, Poicebot —
>The air was full of women,
>>And Savairic Mauleon
>Gave him his land and knight's fee, and he wed the woman.

Postcard: Mauléon-Barousse — Place du Pont et la Tour.

Mauléon was the seat of Savairic de Mauléon (d. 1236), a French warrior and troubadour whose loyalty vacillated between Henry III of England and Louis VIII of France (Edwards & Vaase, p. 140).

In *Literary Essays* (195-96) Pound provides his own Englished *razo* of Gaubertz de Poicebot, a monk who became a troubadour and whose desire of woman made him leave his cloister. He was received and rewarded by Savairic de Mauléon, who knighted him and gave him land so he might win the woman he loved. The passage in Canto V is a condensation of that prose narrative.

(50) Postcard: Mauléon-Barousse — Le Château et l'Eglise.

(51)
>He loved this lady in castle Montaignac?
>The castle flanked him — he had need of it.
>You read to-day, how long the overlords of Perigord,
>The Talleyrands, have held the place; it was no transient fiction.

Postcard: Montignac — Ruines due Château Féodal.

(52)
>>Let us say we see
>En Bertrans, a tower-room at Hautefort,
>Sunset, the ribbon-like road lies, in red cross-light,
>Southward toward Montaignac . . .

Postcard: Château de Hautefort (Dordogne) — Monument historique où naquit le fameux Troubador Bertrand de Born en 1145. Bâti au XI siècle, reconstruit au XVI s. Entrée du Château.

In an article entitled "On 'Near Perigord' " for Poetry VII (3rd December 1915) Pound wrote: 'As to the possibility of a political intrigue behind the apparent love poem we have no evidence save that offered by my own observation of the geography of Perigord and Limoges.' (Ruthven, p. 179).

(53) Verso of a postcard of le Château de Hautefort but sent from Montignac to Mrs. H. Shakespear by Dorothy Pound.

'Aug. 2 at Montignac. We spent last night at Altaforte — & started out soon after 6 a.m. for here. Déj. here & dinner & on a short way by train. It was a lovely walk about 16 miles over highish hills — This was where Bertrand de Born's "Maint" lived. — Last night we slept close to where Henry II's men probably camped, besieging B. de Born. D.'

(54) QUIA PAUPER | AMAVI | EZRA POUND | LONDON: THE EGOIST LTD. | 23 ADELPHI TERRACE HOUSE, W.C.2.

This is copy No. V and bears Ezra Pound's signature. The fly-leaf bears the inscription 'D.P. her book' in his handwriting. On a postcard of Toulouse — Cours Dillon — Le Pont-Neuf sent to Mrs. Shakespear, 7th June 1919, EP announced, 'Proofs of Egoist vol. finished today.'

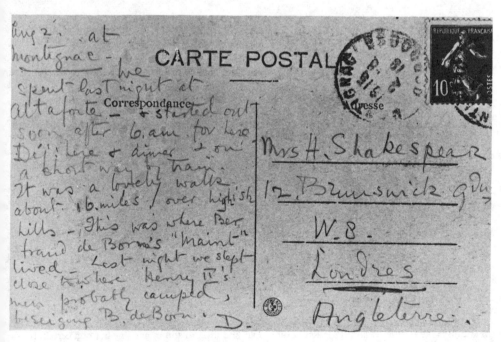

Exhibit No. 53 from the Exhibition catalogue.

(55) EXULTATIONS | OF | EZRA POUND | (*device* in orange-red) London | ELKIN MATHEWS, VIGO STREET | MCMIX.

The fly-leaf bears the inscription: 'Olivia Shakespear, 1909' in her hand.

(56) (*In black*) THE | (*in red*) SPRIT OF ROMANCE | (*in black*) AN ATTEMPT TO DEFINE SOMEWHAT THE | CHARM OF THE PRE-RENAISSANCE | LITERATURE OF LATIN EUROPE | BY | EZRA POUND, M.A. | AUTHOR OF "PERSONAE" AND "EXULTATIONS" (*device*) LONDON | (*in red*) J. M. DENT & SONS, LTD. | (*in black*) 29 AND 30 BEDFORD STREET, W.C.

This edition does not contain the present chapter V "Psychology and Troubadours", first published in *Quest* (October 1912). It was incorporated in the 1932 and subsequent reprintings.

This copy bears the inscription 'O. Shakespear June 1910 (from E.P.)' on the fly-leaf and on a following blank page Pound has copied down Metastasio's poem *L'eta d'oro*.

Shown here is one of EP's early Provençal translations, part verse, part prose: Peire Vidal's Song of Breath — 'Ab l'alen tir vas me l'aire'. (pp. 44-45)

(57) PROVENCA | POEMS | SELECTED FROM PERSONAE, | EXULTATIONS, AND | CANZONIERE | OF | EZRA POUND | (*device*) | BOSTON | SMALL, MAYNARD AND COMPANY | PUBLISHERS.

The fly-leaf bears the inscription 'Mistress Dorothy Shakespear' in EP's hand. On the cover he has drawn attention to the publisher's responsibility for its colour.

(58) SONNETS AND | BALLATE OF | GUIDO CAVALCANTI | WITH TRANSLATIONS | OF THEM AND AN | INTRODUCTION BY | EZRA POUND | (*device*) | MCXII | STEPHEN SWIFT AND CO., LTD. | 16 KING STREET, COVENT GARDEN | LONDON.

The dedication reads: 'As much of this book as is mine I send to my friends Violet and Ford Madox Hueffer.'

In his "Introduction" Pound has put forward this poetic credo which helps us to see the importance that Cavalcanti had for him: 'As for the verse itself: I believe in an ultimate and absolute rhythm as I believe in an absolute symbol or metaphor. The perception of the intellect is given in the word, that of the emotions in the cadence. It is only, then, in perfect rhythm joined to the perfect word that the two-fold vision can be recorded.'

According to Gallup (p. 137) 'the bulk of this edition was destroyed by fire.' These translations along with the original poems in Italian by Cavalcanti are re-printed in *The Translations*.

(59) CATHAY | TRANSLATIONS BY | EZRA POUND | FOR THE MOST PART FROM THE CHINESE | OF RIHAKU, FROM THE NOTES OF THE | LATE ERNEST FENOLLOSA, AND | THE DECIPHERINGS OF | THE PROFESSORS MORI | AND ARIGA. | (*ornament*) | LONDON | ELKIN MATHEWS, CORK STREET | MCMXV.

Pound supplies a note at the end of this volume which was not subsequently reprinted with later collections containing *Cathay*.

'I have not come to the end of Ernest Fenollosa's notes by a long way, nor is it entirely perplexity that causes me to cease from translation. True, I can find little to add to one line out of a certain poem:

> "You know well where it was that I walked
> When you had left me."

In another I find a perfect speech in a literality which will be to many most unacceptable. The couplet is as follows:

> "Drawing sword, cut into water, water again flow:
> Raise cup, quench sorrow, sorrow again sorry."

There are also other poems, notably the "Five Colour Screen", in which Professor Fenollosa was, as an art critic, especially interested, and Rihaku's sort of Ars Poetica, which might be given with diffidence to an audience of good-will. But if I give them, with the necessary breaks for explanation, and a tedium of notes, it is quite certain that the personal hatred in which I am held by many, and the *invidia* which is directed against me because I have dared openly to declare my belief in certain young artists, will be brought to bear first on the flaws of such translation, and will then be merged into depreciation of the whole book of translations. Therefore I give only these unquestionable poems.'

(60) Photograph of Dorothy Pound in the 1920's. Taken in Walter Rummel's flat in Paris? (Walter Morse Rummel edited *Hesternae Rosae* which was published in 1913. This was a collection of XIIth and XIIIth century troubadour songs with piano accompaniment and with French and English translations. EP assisted in the choice of the poems and prepared English versions. Rummel was an American composer and musician whose playing of Debussy's piano works was highly praised by Debussy himself. 'Maestro de Tocar' in *Canzoni* (1911) is dedicated to him and he and his playing are again evoked at the beginning of *Canto LXXX*. The Pounds often stayed in his flat when they were in Paris).

(61) Photograph of Ezra Pound, *circa* 1914 (Mansell collection).

(62) Photograph of Ezra Pound in the 1920's; France and Italy.

(63) Photograph of Ezra Pound in Rapallo, the 1930's, with a sculpture by Gaudier-Brzeska (Culver Pictures, Inc., New York).

(64) Photograph of Ezra Pound in the late 1960's.

(65) Photograph of Ezra Pound and Walter Pilkington, Librarian of Hamilton College, New York, and one of the trustees of the Ezra Pound Literary Trust. This picture was taken on the occasion of the conferring of an honorary degree on James Laughlin of New Directions, (Hamilton College, June 1969).

(66) Pen and ink drawing of Ezra Pound by Wyndham Lewis, 1914.

Private Collection.

train today t Brive. Have hed three long wonderful walkes

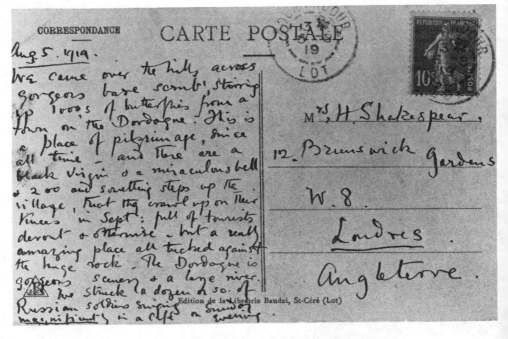

Edition de la Librairie Baudel, St-Céré (Lot)

Postcard: Rocamadour (Lot), August 5, 1919.